TRAVEL GUIDE

Table of Contents

1   Introduction 5

   1.1   Map of Mozambique 7

   1.2   Map of Africa 8

   1.3   A Journey through Time: History of Mozambique 9

   1.4   The Population of Mozambique 10

   1.5   Languages of Mozambique and common phrases 11

   1.6   The culture of Mozambique 12

   1.7   Currency in Mozambique 16

   1.8   Geography and Climate of Mozambique 17

   1.9   Best time to visit Mozambique 18

   1.10   Key attractions in Mozambique 19

   1.11   Interesting facts about Mozambique 20

   1.12   FAQ's when travelling to Mozambique 22

   1.13   Safety precautions 23

2   Getting to Mozambique 25

   2.1   Visa requirements and Entry Regulations 25

   2.2   Traveling to Mozambique 26

   2.3   Transport from the airports 26

   2.4   Public transportation 28

   2.5   Car Rentals and Driving 29

   2.6   Tour Companies 31

   2.7   Other means of getting around 32

3   Where to stay in Mozambique 34

   3.1   Districts in Mozambique 34

   3.2   Hotels in Maputo, Mozambique 35

3.3	Hotels in Beira, Mozambique	38
3.4	Hotels in Tofo and Barra	41
3.5	Food Culture of Mozambique	44
3.6	Traditional Food from Mozambique	46
3.7	Restaurants	47
3.8	Markets	49
4	Top Attractions in Mozambique	51
4.1	Maputo, The Heart of Mozambique	51
4.2	Historical Landmarks	51
4.3	The Maputo Fortress	51
4.4	Cultural Attractions	51
4.5	Natural Attractions	51
4.6	Food and Markets	52
4.7	Gorongosa National Park	54
4.8	Bazaruto Archipelago	55
4.9	Ilha de Mozambique: A Historical Gem	57
4.10	Inhambane: A Coastal Paradise	59
4.11	Pemba: A Tropical Haven	61
4.12	Niassa Reserve: A Wildlife Wonderland	62
4.13	Quirimbas Archipelago: A Tropical Paradise	63
4.14	Chimanimani Mountains: A Hiker's Paradise	64
4.15	Swimming with Dolphins	66
5	Culture and Entertainment in Mozambique	67
5.1	Art Galleries	67
5.2	Museums	68
5.3	Theatres	69
5.4	Nightlife in Mozambique	69
5.5	Shopping in Mozambique	70

6   Day Trips and Excursions 72

    6.1   One Day tour of Maputo....................................72

    6.2   One-day Beach Escape in Tofo............................74

    6.3   One-day Wildlife Adventure in Gorongosa National Park ...76

    6.4   One-day Historical Journey in Ilha de Mozambique 78

    6.5   From Maputo: Day trip to Ponta do Oura....................80

    6.6   Maputo: Highlights Tour with Local Beer Tasting:...............83

7   Two-Day Maputo and Inhaca Island Adventure 85

    7.1   Day One: Maputo....................................85

    7.2   Day 2: Inhaca Island Adventure 87

8   Three-Day Maputo and Tofo Beach Getaway....................89

    8.1   Day One: Maputo....................................89

    8.2   Day 2: Travel to Tofo Beach 91

    8.3   Day 3: Tofo Beach Adventure 91

9   Practical Tips for Visiting Mozambique....................95

    9.1   Health and Safety....................................95

    9.2   Currency....................................95

    9.3   Language....................................95

    9.4   Clothing....................................95

    9.5   Transportation 95

    9.6   Respect Local Customs 96

    9.7   Security 96

    9.8   Food and Water 96

10   Conclusion 97

1   Introduction

Welcome to Mozambique, a hidden gem nestled along the southeastern coastline of Africa. A land of contrasts and surprises, Mozambique is a destination that promises an unforgettable journey for those who dare to venture off the beaten path.

Mozambique is a country that dances to the rhythm of its own drum, a place where the spirit of Africa meets the tranquility of the Indian Ocean. With over 2,500 kilometers of pristine coastline, it is a paradise for beach lovers and marine enthusiasts. The turquoise waters are home to a vibrant array of marine life, making it a world-class destination for scuba diving, snorkeling, and fishing. The untouched coral reefs of the Bazaruto and Quirimbas Archipelagos are teeming with colorful fish, manta rays, and even the elusive dugong.

But the allure of Mozambique extends far beyond its beaches. Venture inland, and you'll discover a land rich in culture and history. The country's past is a tapestry woven with threads of Arab, African, and European influences. This is evident in the architecture of the capital city, Maputo, where modern buildings stand side by side with colonial-era Portuguese structures. The city's vibrant arts scene, bustling markets, and lively nightlife make it a must-visit urban destination.

In the north, the Island of Mozambique, a UNESCO World Heritage Site, tells tales of a bygone era. Once a major hub on the spice route, the island is steeped in history, with its fortresses, palaces, and chapels bearing witness to the passage of time.

Mozambique's cultural diversity is reflected in its cuisine. A fusion of African, Portuguese, and Arab flavors, Mozambican food is a gastronomic delight. From the national dish, Matapa, a succulent stew of cassava leaves, garlic, and coconut milk, to the mouth-watering seafood platters served on the beach, dining in Mozambique is an experience in itself.

Nature lovers will not be disappointed either. The country's national parks, such as Gorongosa and Niassa, offer exceptional wildlife viewing opportunities. From elephants and lions to unique bird species, these parks are a testament to Mozambique's commitment to conservation.

Yet, what truly sets Mozambique apart is its people. Warm, welcoming, and resilient, the Mozambicans are the heart and soul of the country. Their infectious smiles, rhythmic music, and vibrant traditional dances, like the Marrabenta and Mapiko, encapsulate the spirit of Mozambique - a spirit of joy, resilience, and hope.

Visiting Mozambique is not just about seeing a new place. It's about immersing yourself in a rich cultural experience, connecting with nature, and making memories that will last a lifetime. It's about feeling the warm sand between your toes as you watch the sun set over the Indian Ocean, listening to the hauntingly beautiful call of the African Fish Eagle, tasting the fiery heat of peri-peri prawns, and dancing to the rhythm of traditional Mozambican music under a starlit sky.

Mozambique is a country that has faced its share of challenges, but it is also a country that refuses to be defined by them. It is a country that embraces the future without forgetting the past. It is a country that invites you to explore, to discover, and to fall in love with its beauty, its people, and its spirit.

So, come to Mozambique. Come for the adventure, stay for the unforgettable experiences, and leave with a piece of Africa in your heart. Your journey awaits.

1.1 Map of Mozambique

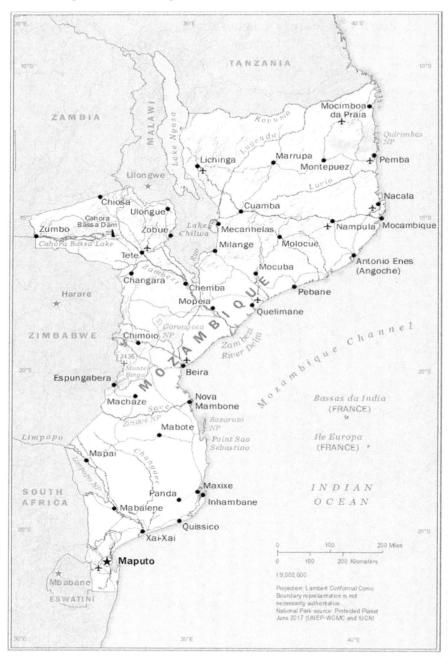

1.2 Map of Africa

The map below indicates the location of Mozambique in the continent of Africa.

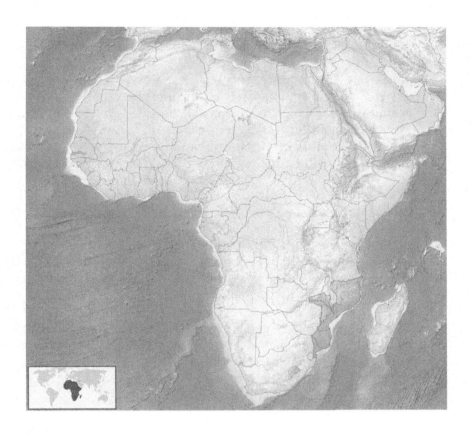

1.3 A Journey through Time: History of Mozambique

Mozambique, located in Southeast Africa, has a rich and complex history that spans several centuries. The area was inhabited by Bantu-speaking tribes for thousands of years before the arrival of Arab and Persian traders in the 10th century, who established trading posts along the coast. The region was known for its gold, ivory, and slaves, which were traded across the Indian Ocean.

In the late 15th century, Portuguese explorers led by Vasco da Gama arrived in Mozambique. The Portuguese established forts and trading posts along the coast, and by the 16th century, they had gained control of the trade routes in the Indian Ocean. The Portuguese influence in Mozambique grew over the centuries, and by the 19th century, the region was considered a Portuguese colony.

The colonial period was marked by exploitation and forced labor. Many Mozambicans were forced to work in the plantations and mines of the Portuguese. The colonial rule was also marked by significant economic development, particularly in the cash crop sector. However, the benefits of this development were largely enjoyed by the Portuguese, while the local population suffered from poverty and neglect.

The struggle for independence in Mozambique began in the early 20th century. The main force behind the independence movement was the Mozambique Liberation Front (FRELIMO), which was formed in 1962. FRELIMO launched a guerrilla war against the Portuguese, which lasted for over a decade.

Mozambique gained independence from Portugal in 1975. However, the country was soon plunged into a brutal civil war between FRELIMO, which had taken over the government, and the Mozambican National Resistance (RENAMO), a rebel group supported by Rhodesia (now Zimbabwe) and South Africa. The civil war lasted for 15 years and resulted in the death of a million people and the displacement of millions more.

The civil war ended in 1992 with a peace agreement brokered by the United Nations. Since then, Mozambique has made significant strides in political and economic reform. The country has held multiple rounds of peaceful elections and has experienced steady economic growth.

However, Mozambique still faces significant challenges. The country is one of the poorest in the world, and it struggles with high rates of poverty, unemployment, and inequality. In recent years, the country has also been plagued by a resurgence of conflict, with RENAMO and a new insurgent group in the northern province of Cabo Delgado launching attacks against the government.

1.4 The Population of Mozambique

Mozambique, officially known as the Republic of Mozambique, is a country located in Southeast Africa. It is bordered by the Indian Ocean to the east and several countries including Tanzania, Malawi, Zambia, Zimbabwe, Swaziland, and South Africa. The country has a diverse culture and history that is reflected in its population.

As of the latest estimates, the population of Mozambique is approximately 31.26 million people. The country has a relatively young population, with a median age of 17.8 years. The population growth rate is around 2.93%, which is one of the highest in the world. This high growth rate is primarily due to the country's high fertility rate, which is around 4.9 children per woman.

The capital of Mozambique is Maputo, which is also the largest city in the country. Maputo is home to approximately 1.1 million people. The city is the country's cultural, economic, and political hub, hosting many important institutions and landmarks. Other major cities in Mozambique include Matola, Beira, and Nampula. Matola, located near Maputo, is the second-largest city with a population of around 675,422 people. Beira, with a population of about 431,583 people, is the largest port in the country and serves as a gateway for both the central and northern regions of the country. Nampula, in the northern part of the country, is the third-largest city with a population of approximately 743,125 people.

Mozambique is a country of great ethnic diversity. The population is primarily made up of various Bantu-speaking ethnic groups. The largest ethnic group is the Makua, but there are numerous other groups including the Tsonga, Shangaan, Lomwe, Sena, and Ndau.

There is also a smaller population of Europeans, mainly of Portuguese descent, as well as some Indian and Pakistani communities.

The official language of Mozambique is Portuguese, which is spoken by about 50.3% of the population. However, there are several indigenous languages that are widely spoken, including Makhuwa, Sena, and Tsonga. The country is predominantly Christian, with a significant Muslim minority.

In terms of health, Mozambique faces several challenges. The life expectancy is relatively low, with men living an average of 52.6 years and women living an average of 55.3 years. The country has a high infant mortality rate and a high maternal mortality rate. HIV/AIDS is prevalent, affecting about 12.6% of the population.

Despite these challenges, Mozambique has made significant strides in recent years. The government has implemented various programs aimed at improving health, education, and economic opportunities. The country has a growing economy, with agriculture, manufacturing, and services being the main sectors.

In conclusion, Mozambique is a country of rich cultural diversity with a rapidly growing population. Despite facing several challenges, the country is making progress in improving the quality of life for its people.

1.5 Languages of Mozambique and common phrases

Mozambique is a melting pot of languages, reflecting its rich cultural diversity. The official language is Portuguese, a legacy of the colonial period, and it is spoken by about 47.3% of all Mozambicans aged 5 and older. However, it's important to note that native Portuguese speakers make up only 16.6% of the population. Portuguese is more commonly spoken in urban areas and is used as a second language by many.

In addition to Portuguese, there are a number of Bantu languages indigenous to Mozambique. These include Makhuwa, Sena, Tsonga, Lomwe, and Shona, among others. Makhuwa is the most widely spoken local language, with over 7 million speakers. Other significant languages include Xichangana, Nyanja, Ndau, and Sena.

The language of the deaf community in Mozambique is Mozambican Sign Language.

Interestingly, most Mozambicans are multilingual, speaking more than one language. This multilingualism is reflected in the country's education system, with primary education becoming fully bilingual in 2017, including 16 Mozambican languages, followed by Portuguese as a foreign language.

Small communities of Arabs, Chinese, and Indians also reside in Mozambique, speaking their own languages aside from Portuguese as their second language. For instance, Indians from Portuguese India speak any of the Portuguese Creoles of their origin.

As a tourist, knowing a few common phrases in Portuguese can be helpful. Here are some to get you started.
- "Bom dia" - Good morning
- "Boa tarde" - Good afternoon
- "Boa noite" - Good evening or Good night
- "Obrigado" (male) / "Obrigada" (female) - Thank you
- "Por favor" - Please
- "Desculpe" - Sorry
- "Sim" - Yes
- "Não" - No
- "Não entendo" - I don't understand
- "Fala inglês?" - Do you speak English?
-

Remember, a little effort goes a long way and locals appreciate when visitors make an attempt to speak their language. It's a great way to show respect and interest in their culture. Happy travels!

1.6   The culture of Mozambique

Culture of Mozambique

Mozambique, located in Southeast Africa, is a nation rich in cultural diversity, with a complex blend of indigenous, colonial, and modern influences. The culture of Mozambique is a reflection of its history, with influences from Bantu-speaking tribes, Arab traders, Portuguese colonizers, and other African nations.

The culture of Mozambique is largely derived from its history of Bantu, Swahili, and Portuguese rule, and has expanded since independence in 1975. The majority of its inhabitants are black Africans, and its main language is Portuguese. Mozambique has a rich history in the areas of arts, cuisine, and entertainment.

The main ethnic groups in Mozambique are Makhuwa, Tsonga, Makonde, Shangaan, Shona, Sena, Ndau, and other indigenous groups. There are approximately 45,000 Europeans, and 15,000 South Asians. The main religious groups in Mozambique are Christian (57%), Muslim (20%), Indigenous African, and other beliefs.

The country's cultural heritage is evident in its music, dance, and art. Traditional music in Mozambique includes Marrabenta and Timbila, both of which are popular forms of music and dance. Marrabenta is a genre of music that originated in the 1930s and is characterized by its lively rhythm and dance style. Timbila, on the other hand, is a traditional form of music and dance performed by the Chopi people of southern Mozambique. The Chopi people are known for their intricate xylophone music, which is often accompanied by a dance.

Mozambique's art scene is also vibrant, with the Makonde people being renowned for their intricate wood carvings. These carvings often depict human figures and are deeply rooted in local traditions and beliefs. In addition to traditional art forms, Mozambique is also home to a burgeoning contemporary art scene.

Languages

The official language is Portuguese, English is sometimes spoken in major cities such as Maputo and Beira. According to the 2007 census, 50.4% of the national population aged 5 and older (80.8% of people living in urban areas and 36.3% in rural areas) is fluent in Portuguese, making it the most widely spoken language in the country. The other languages spoken in Mozambique include Emakhuwa (at 25.3%), Xichangana (at 10.3%), Cisena (at 7.5%), Elomwe (at 7%), Echuwabo (at 5.1%), and a variety of other languages.

Religion and Education
Religion plays a significant role in the lives of many Mozambicans. The country is predominantly Christian, with a significant Muslim minority. According to the 2007 census, about 56.1% of the population is Christian, 17.9% is Muslim, and 7.3% adheres to traditional beliefs. However, the actual numbers may vary as many people practice syncretic forms of religion, combining elements of Christianity or Islam with traditional African beliefs.
Christianity arrived in Mozambique with the Portuguese colonizers in the 15th century. The Roman Catholic Church is the largest Christian denomination in the country, followed by various Protestant denominations, including the Anglican, Baptist, and Methodist churches.

Islam in Mozambique is primarily Sunni and has been present in the country since the Arab traders arrived on the East African coast. The majority of Muslims live in the north of the country, particularly in the coastal strip.

Traditional African religions are also practiced in Mozambique, particularly in rural areas. These religions often involve ancestor worship and belief in spirits. Despite the prevalence of Christianity and Islam, traditional beliefs continue to influence many aspects of Mozambican life, including social norms, rituals, and the understanding of illness and healing.

Arts and Entertainment
The music of Mozambique can serve many purposes, ranging from religious expression to traditional ceremonies. Musical instruments are usually handmade. Some of the instruments used in Mozambican musical expression include drums made of wood and animal skin; the lupembe, a woodwind instrument made from animal horns or

wood; and the marimba, which is a kind of xylophone native to Mozambique.

The Makonde are renowned for their wood carving and elaborate masks that are commonly used in ritual dances. There are two different kinds of wood carvings. Shetani (evil spirits), which are mostly carved in heavy ebony, tall, and elegantly curved with symbols and nonrepresentational faces. The ujamaa are totem-type carvings which illustrate lifelike faces of people and various figures. These sculptures are usually referred to as "family trees" because they tell stories of many generations.

Dances are usually intricate, highly developed traditions throughout Mozambique. There are many different kinds of dances from tribe to tribe which are usually ritualistic in nature. The Chopi, for instance, act out battles dressed in animal skins. The men of Makua dress in colourful outfits and masks while dancing on stilts around the village for hours. Groups of women in the northern part of the country perform a traditional dance called tufo, to celebrate Islamic holidays.

Cuisine
Mozambican cuisine is rich and varied, reflecting both its traditional roots as well as outside influences. Flavourful spicy stews eaten with rice or steamed cornmeal dough are common. With its long coastline and rich fishing presence, fish is a key part of the national diet. The country is famous for its shellfish, such as prawns and crayfish, and its combination of seafood dishes with the spicy piri-piri sauce (which literally translates to "Spicy-Spicy").

One particular stew that is without Portuguese influence is matapa, which is usually made with cassava leaves, cashews, crab, shrimp and coconut milk. Another important dish is piri-piri chicken, which is grilled chicken basted in piri-piri sauce and served with fries.
Like its African neighbors, Mozambique is also blessed with a wide variety of fruits, including citrus produce (such as oranges and grapefruit), bananas, mangoes and coconuts which are enjoyed throughout the nation.

Cultural Identity
Mozambique was ruled by Portugal and they share in common; main language and second main religion (Roman Catholicism). But since most of the people are Bantus, most of the culture is native and for

Bantus living in urban areas with some Portuguese influence. Mozambican culture influences the Portuguese culture. The music, movies (by RTP África), food, and traditions are now part of everyday lifestyles of Portugal.

Spirit Possession

A new phenomenon of spirit possession appeared after the Mozambican Civil War. These spirits, called gamba, are identified as dead soldiers, and overwhelmingly possess women. Prior to the war, spirit possession was limited to certain families and was less common.

1.7 Currency in Mozambique

The currency used in Mozambique is the Mozambican Metical (MZN). The Metical is subdivided into 100 centavos. The currency symbol for the Metical is MT, and its ISO code is MZN. The Mozambican Metical was introduced in 1980 as a replacement for the Mozambican Escudo.

Methods of Payment

When it comes to making payments in Mozambique, it's important to note that credit cards are not widely accepted outside of major cities and tourist areas. Therefore, it's advisable to carry cash, especially when traveling to remote areas. ATMs are available in cities and larger towns, and they usually offer the best exchange rates. However, it's important to be aware of potential fraud and to use ATMs in secure locations.

Money Exchange

Exchanging money can be done at banks, hotels, and authorized exchange bureaus. It's recommended to avoid black market exchanges due to the risk of counterfeit money and potential legal issues. It's also important to keep all exchange receipts, as you may need them to convert Meticals back to your home currency upon departure.

Withdrawing Cash

As for withdrawing cash, it's possible to do so at ATMs using a Visa card. However, MasterCard and American Express are not widely accepted. It's also worth noting that there may be withdrawal limits and fees, so it's advisable to check with your bank before traveling.

Regarding the exchange rate, as of the time of this search, 1 US Dollar is approximately equivalent to 63.50 Mozambican Metical, 1 Euro is approximately equivalent to 74.90 Mozambican Metical, and 1 British Pound is approximately equivalent to 87.70 Mozambican Metical. Please note that exchange rates fluctuate constantly due to market conditions, so it's important to check for the most current rates before making any transactions.

1.8   Geography and Climate of Mozambique

Geography of Mozambique
Mozambique is located in southeastern Africa, and it is bordered by the Indian Ocean to the east and Tanzania to the north. The country also shares borders with Malawi and Zambia to the northwest, Zimbabwe to the west, and Eswatini (Swaziland) and South Africa to the southwest. The country covers an area of 801,590 square kilometers, making it the world's 36th largest country.
The country's geography is diverse, with coastal lowlands in the east and high plateaus in the west. The Zambezi River divides the country into northern and southern regions. The northern region is characterized by highlands, deep valleys, and large rivers, while the southern region is mainly low-lying coastal areas with swamps, small lakes, and lagoons. The highest point in Mozambique is Mount Binga at 2,436 meters above sea level, located in the western part of the country.

Climate of Mozambique
Mozambique has a tropical climate, with two distinct seasons: a wet season from November to March and a dry season from April to October. The country's climate varies from tropical and subtropical in the south to tropical and equatorial in the north. The coastal areas are warm and humid throughout the year, with temperatures averaging between 27°C and 29°C. The interior highlands are cooler, with temperatures averaging between 19°C and 26°C.

The wet season is characterized by heavy rainfall, particularly in the highlands. The country is prone to severe weather events, including cyclones and floods, particularly during the wet season. The dry season is generally cooler and less humid, making it the best time for tourism.

Despite its tropical location, Mozambique's climate is not uniformly hot and humid. The country's diverse geography results in significant climatic variations, with cooler temperatures in the highlands and warmer temperatures along the coast. The country's climate and geography make it rich in biodiversity, with a wide range of flora and fauna.

1.9   Best time to visit Mozambique

Best Times to Visit Mozambique
The best time to visit Mozambique is between September and November. During these months, the game viewing is at its peak, whale migration can be observed, and the weather is calm and warm, with temperatures ranging between 81°F to 90°F. This period offers a great opportunity for wildlife enthusiasts and those interested in marine life.

Mozambique has a subtropical climate. The dry season lasts from April to December, with temperatures between 77°F and 90°F. This is an ideal time for beach lovers as the beaches on both the Bazaruto and Quirimbas archipelagos are stunning throughout the dry season. However, the winter months (June to August) can be breezy, especially in the north, so it's something to keep in mind if you're planning a beach vacation.

Many people visit Mozambique in July and August, but September and October are particularly recommended for diving and snorkeling enthusiasts as the conditions are at their best and the weather is gloriously sunny and calm.

Visiting Mozambique in July
July is winter in Mozambique and the heart of the dry season, which brings clear, warm, and sunny days. This is also a very pleasant month for sightseeing at Ibo or in the country's vibrant capital, Maputo. It can be windy on the northern beaches, so if you're planning a beach holiday, you might want to consider this.

Stunning Sightseeing Weather (May to September)
During these months the air is clear and pleasant in Ibo, Ilha de Mozambique, and Maputo, making it an excellent time to do some sightseeing.

Humpback Whale Migration (June to November)
Whale watching opportunities abound during these months as humpback whales make their epic annual migration from Antarctica to warmer waters off East Africa to have their young. This is a spectacle not to be missed if you're visiting during this period.

In conclusion, the best time to visit Mozambique largely depends on the activities you're interested in. Whether it's wildlife viewing, beach relaxation, diving, snorkeling, or sightseeing, there's a perfect time for you to experience the best of what Mozambique has to offer.

1.10 Key attractions in Mozambique

Here are some of the key attractions in Mozambique.

Maputo
Maputo, the capital of Mozambique, is a bustling city known for its Portuguese colonial architecture and vibrant cultural scene. The city is home to the Maputo Railway Station, an architectural landmark, and the Fortress of Maputo, a historical military site. The city's vibrant markets, such as the Mercado Central, offer a variety of local goods and produce.

Gorongosa National Park
Gorongosa National Park is one of the country's main tourist attractions. It's a wildlife lover's paradise, home to diverse species including elephants, lions, and zebras. The park is also known for its conservation efforts.

Bazaruto Archipelago
The Bazaruto Archipelago is a group of six islands off the coast of Mozambique. It's a popular destination for diving and snorkeling, with clear waters and abundant marine life. The archipelago is also home to the Bazaruto National Park.

Ilha de Mozambique
Ilha de Mozambique is a UNESCO World Heritage Site known for its colonial architecture. The island was a major Arab port and boat building center in the years before Vasco de Gama visited in 1498. The Chapel of Nossa Senhora de Baluarte, built in 1522, is considered the oldest European building in the southern hemisphere.

Inhambane
Inhambane is one of the oldest settlements on Mozambique's east coast. The city is known for its Portuguese colonial architecture and nearby beaches. The Cathedral of Our Lady of Conception is a notable landmark, and visitors can climb to the top of the spire for a panoramic view of the city.

Pemba
Pemba is a port city in northern Mozambique known for its beaches, including Wimbe Beach. The city is also a popular base for diving and snorkeling trips to the Quirimbas Archipelago.

Niassa Reserve
Niassa Reserve is the largest conservation area in Mozambique, covering parts of the Niassa and Cabo Delgado Provinces. The reserve is home to significant wildlife populations, including elephants, lions, and African wild dogs.

Quirimbas Archipelago
The Quirimbas Archipelago is a group of about 30 islands that stretch along the northern coast of Mozambique. The islands are known for their coral reefs, mangroves, and beaches. The Quirimbas National Park covers much of the archipelago and mainland.

Lake Niassa
Lake Niassa, also known as Lake Malawi, is the third largest and second deepest lake in Africa. The Mozambican side of the lake is less developed than the Malawian side, offering pristine beaches and clear waters.

Chimanimani Mountains
The Chimanimani Mountains straddle the border between Zimbabwe and Mozambique. The mountains are known for their dramatic peaks, deep valleys, and diverse flora and fauna. The region is popular for hiking and bird watching.

Please note that the information provided is a brief summary and for more detailed information, you may want to visit the respective places or their official websites.

1.11 Interesting facts about Mozambique

Below are some interesting and lesser-known facts about Mozambique.

Geographical Diversity

Mozambique is a country of great geographical diversity. It is located in southeastern Africa and is bordered by six countries: Tanzania, Malawi, Zambia, Zimbabwe, South Africa, and Eswatini. It also has a coastline along the Indian Ocean, which is about 2,470 kilometers long. The country's landscape varies from coastal lowlands to mountainous regions, providing a variety of ecosystems and wildlife.

Cultural Richness

Mozambique is rich in culture, with a mix of Bantu, Swahili, and Portuguese influences. The official language is Portuguese, but there are many indigenous languages spoken throughout the country. The country is also known for its traditional music and dance, particularly the style known as Marrabenta, and the traditional dance called Mapiko.

Historical Significance

Mozambique has a rich history, with evidence of human habitation dating back to the Stone Age. The country was colonized by Portugal in the 16th century and gained independence in 1975. The post-independence period was marked by a long civil war that lasted from 1977 to 1992.

Economic Potential

Despite facing many challenges, Mozambique has significant economic potential. It has abundant natural resources, including coal and natural gas. The country also has potential for growth in the tourism sector, with its beautiful beaches, wildlife reserves, and historical sites.

Famous Visitors

Mozambique has been visited by many famous people over the years. One of the most notable is former South African president Nelson Mandela, who had a holiday home on the island of Inhaca. The island is now a popular tourist destination.

Unique Cuisine

Mozambique's cuisine is as diverse as its culture, with influences from Portugal, India, and the Middle East. The country is particularly known for its seafood, with dishes like Prawns à la Moçambique, which is prawns cooked in a sauce of garlic, onion, and chili.

Interesting Wildlife

Mozambique is home to a wide variety of wildlife, including elephants, lions, and over 500 bird species. The country's national animal is the African elephant, and the Gorongosa National Park is one of the best

places to see these majestic creatures in their natural habitat.

The Flag

Mozambique's flag is unique as it is the only national flag in the world to feature a modern assault rifle, specifically an AK-47. It is a symbol of the country's struggle for independence.

These are just a few of the many fascinating aspects of Mozambique. The country is a vibrant mix of cultures, history, and natural beauty, making it a fascinating place to explore.

1.12 FAQ's when travelling to Mozambique

Below are some frequently asked questions (FAQs) and their answers that a first-time visitor to Mozambique might find helpful.

What is the official language of Mozambique?

The official language of Mozambique is Portuguese. However, English is widely spoken in tourist areas, hotels, and by guides. There are also numerous local languages spoken throughout the country.

What currency is used in Mozambique?

The official currency of Mozambique is the Mozambican Metical (MZN). Credit cards are accepted in most hotels and restaurants in cities, but it's a good idea to have some local currency for smaller establishments and local markets.

Do I need a visa to travel to Mozambique?

Visa requirements for Mozambique vary depending on your nationality. It's best to check with the Mozambique embassy or consulate in your home country before your trip. As of my knowledge cutoff in September 2021, many nationalities can obtain a visa on arrival, but this could change.

Is it safe to travel to Mozambique?
As with any travel destination, it's important to stay informed about current conditions and take precautions. Petty crime can occur, particularly in crowded areas. Always keep an eye on your belongings and avoid displaying expensive items. In general, Mozambicans are friendly and welcoming to tourists.

What is the best time to visit Mozambique?
The best time to visit Mozambique is during the dry season, from April to September. The weather during this time is generally warm and dry, making it ideal for wildlife viewing and beach activities.

What vaccinations do I need before traveling to Mozambique?
It's recommended to be up-to-date on routine vaccines before traveling to Mozambique. Additionally, vaccines for diseases like Hepatitis A and Typhoid are also recommended. Malaria is present in Mozambique, so antimalarial medication may be necessary. Always consult with a healthcare provider before your trip.

What kind of power plugs and sockets are used in Mozambique?
Mozambique uses type C, F, and M plugs. The standard voltage is 220 V, and the standard frequency is 50 Hz. It's a good idea to bring a universal adapter if your devices use different plugs.

What is the food like in Mozambique?
Mozambican cuisine is a blend of African, Portuguese, and Indian influences. Seafood is a staple, particularly prawns. Other common ingredients include maize, rice, and chicken. Piri-piri, a spicy chili sauce, is also a popular addition to many dishes.

What are the top attractions in Mozambique?
Some of the top attractions in Mozambique include the beautiful beaches of the Bazaruto Archipelago, the colonial architecture of Ilha de Mozambique, and the wildlife-rich Gorongosa National Park.

Is tap water safe to drink in Mozambique?
It's generally recommended to avoid drinking tap water in Mozambique. Bottled water is widely available and is the safest choice for drinking and brushing teeth.

1.13 Safety precautions

Safety is paramount when traveling to any new destination. Here are some safety precautions to consider when visiting Mozambique.

Health Precautions
Before traveling, ensure you're up-to-date on routine vaccines. Also, consult with a healthcare provider about additional vaccines you may need, such as Hepatitis A and Typhoid. Malaria is present in Mozambique, so antimalarial medication may be necessary. Always drink bottled water and eat well-cooked food to avoid foodborne illnesses.

Travel Insurance
It's a good idea to have travel insurance that covers medical evacuation, as medical facilities in Mozambique may not be up to the standards you're used to, particularly outside of major cities.

Road Safety
If you're planning to drive, be aware that road conditions can be poor, particularly in rural areas. Avoid driving at night if possible, as roads are often not well lit. Always wear your seatbelt and follow local traffic laws.

Petty Crime
Like many tourist destinations, petty crime such as pickpocketing and bag snatching can occur, particularly in crowded areas. Keep your belongings secure and avoid displaying expensive items like jewelry and cameras. Use hotel safes for your valuables.

Beach Safety
While Mozambique's beaches are beautiful, be aware of strong currents and riptides. Not all beaches have lifeguards, so swim with caution. Also, avoid isolated beaches to reduce the risk of crime.

Respect Local Customs
Mozambique is a diverse country with various cultural norms and traditions. Respect local customs, dress modestly, and be aware of any local laws or regulations.

Stay Informed

Keep up-to-date with the latest travel advisories from your country's foreign affairs department. They provide valuable information about safety and security, health risks, and any areas to avoid.

Emergency Contacts
Keep a list of emergency contacts, including the local police and your nearest embassy or consulate. The general emergency number in Mozambique is 117.

Remember, most visits to Mozambique are trouble-free, and by taking these precautions, you can help ensure a safe and enjoyable trip.

2 Getting to Mozambique

2.1 Visa requirements and Entry Regulations

Here are some guidelines for entry into Mozambique.

Passport
A valid passport is required for travel to Mozambique. Your passport should have a minimum validity of six months from the date you arrive in Mozambique, and it should have at least two blank pages for visa and entry/exit stamps.

Visa Requirements
Visa requirements vary depending on your nationality. As of my knowledge cutoff in September 2021, many nationalities can obtain a visa on arrival in Mozambique. However, it's always best to check with the Mozambique embassy or consulate in your home country before your trip to get the most current information.

COVID-19 Regulations
As of the latest information, a PCR test is no longer needed to enter the country if a person presents a valid certificate showing proof of full vaccination against COVID-19. However, these regulations can change rapidly, so it's important to check the latest updates from reliable sources or your local embassy before your trip.

What Can Be Taken Into the Country
As with any country, there are restrictions on what can be brought into Mozambique. This typically includes restrictions on large

amounts of currency, certain food products, drugs, weapons, and certain animal and plant products. It's best to check with Mozambique's customs regulations for detailed information.

Remember, entry requirements can change, so it's always a good idea to check the latest information from reliable sources before your trip. Enjoy your visit to Mozambique!

For more detailed and updated information, you can visit the following websites:
- o Mozambique International Travel Information - Travel.gov
- o Mozambique - Department of Foreign Affairs - DFA
- o Entry requirements - Mozambique travel advice - GOV.UK

2.2   Traveling to Mozambique

There are several ways to get to Mozambique, depending on where you're coming from and your preferred mode of travel. Here are some options:

By Air
The most common way to reach Mozambique is by air. The country's main international airport is Maputo International Airport, located in the capital city of Maputo. There are direct flights to Maputo from several major cities around the world, including Johannesburg, Lisbon, and Doha. Other international airports in Mozambique include Beira, Nampula, and Pemba.

By Land
If you're in a neighboring country, you might choose to enter Mozambique by land. There are several border crossings with South Africa, Swaziland, Zimbabwe, Zambia, Malawi, and Tanzania. If you're coming from South Africa, you can rent a car in Johannesburg and drive to Maputo. However, be aware that road conditions can vary, and some routes may require a 4x4 vehicle.

By Rail
There's also the option to travel to Mozambique by train. A train runs from Johannesburg and Pretoria to the Mozambique border at Ressano Garcia, where there's a connection to Maputo.

By Sea
While less common, it's also possible to reach Mozambique by sea. Some cruise lines include stops in Mozambique, and there are also cargo ships that accept passengers. However, this option is less frequent and may require more planning.

2.3 Transport from the airports

Here are some examples of means to travel from the airports in Mozambique to the city center.

Maputo International Airport (MPM):
Maputo International Airport is the main international airport in Mozambique, located about 5 km north of the city center.
- o **By Taxi:** Taxis are readily available at the airport. A taxi ride to the city center costs approximately MZN 200 (around USD 10) and takes about 15 minutes.
- o **By Minibus (Chapas):** Minibus taxis, known as chapas, operate along regular routes throughout Maputo. They are a fast and relatively cheap means of getting around the city.
- o **By Airport Transfer Services:** There are also airport transfer services available, such as Taxi2Airport and Shuttle Africa, which you can book in advance. These services offer a range of private vehicles, including cars, minibuses, and luxury options.

Beira Airport (BEW):
Beira Airport is located in Beira, the second largest city in Mozambique.
- o **By Taxi:** Taxis are available at the airport. The fare and travel time will depend on your specific destination in Beira.
- o **By Airport Transfer Services:** As with Maputo, you can book airport transfer services in advance for travel from Beira Airport to your destination in the city.

Nampula Airport (APL) and Pemba Airport (POL):
Nampula and Pemba are other cities in Mozambique with international airports. Similar transportation options are available at these airports, including taxis and pre-booked airport transfer services.

Please note that the costs, frequency, and travel times can vary depending on factors such as traffic conditions and your specific destination in the city. Always confirm the fare with the taxi driver before starting your journey and consider booking airport transfer services in advance for convenience and peace of mind.

2.4 Public transportation

It is important to know how one is going to get around the country. Below is a detailed overview of the public transport system in Mozambique.

Buses
Buses in Mozambique operate between major towns where roads are in good condition. They are a reliable and affordable means of transport, covering all major cities and towns with at least one service a day. However, in rural areas, bus services may be less frequent or unavailable.

Chapas (Minibuses)
Chapas, or minibuses, are a common form of public transport in Mozambique. They operate along regular routes throughout cities and towns, and are a fast and relatively cheap way to get around. However, they can be crowded and may not adhere to a strict

schedule. It's also important to note that chapas may not leave until they are full, which can lead to delays.

Taxis
Taxis are readily available in major cities and towns. They are a convenient but more expensive option. Always confirm the fare with the driver before starting your journey. Some taxis use meters, while others may negotiate a fare upfront.

Payment
Payment for public transport in Mozambique is typically made in cash. It's advisable to have small denominations of the local currency (Mozambican Metical) on hand to pay for fares.

Dos and Don'ts:
- o Do have small change ready for fares.
- o Don't expect buses or chapas to leave on time; they often wait until they are full before departing.
- o Do be aware of your belongings at all times, especially in crowded chapas or bus stations.
- o Don't travel late at night if possible, as public transport services may be less frequent or unavailable.

2.5   Car Rentals and Driving

Should you wish to hire a car, below is a guide on the car rental procedure in Mozambique.

Car Rental Locations
Car rental services are available in major cities and towns, as well as at international airports in Mozambique. Some of the popular car rental companies operating in Mozambique include Sixt, Europcar, and local providers. You can pick up and return the rental car at these locations, or arrange for different pick-up and drop-off points depending on the company's policy.

Documentation Required
To rent a car in Mozambique, you will typically need the following documents:
- o A valid driver's license from your home country.

- An International Driving Permit if your license is not in English.
- A valid passport.
- A credit card in the name of the main driver for the security deposit.

Driving in Mozambique

When driving in Mozambique, keep in mind the following:
- Drive on the left side of the road.
- Seat belts are mandatory for all passengers.
- It's illegal to use a mobile phone while driving unless you have a hands-free system.
- Speed limits are typically 60 km/h in urban areas, 100 km/h on secondary roads, and 120 km/h on motorways.
- Always carry your driving license, passport, and vehicle registration documents while driving.
- Be aware of road conditions, which can be poor especially in rural areas and during the rainy season.

For more detailed information, you can visit the following websites:
- Car Rental in Mozambique | SIXT rent a car: https://www.sixt.com/car-rental/mozambique/
- Mozambique: Terms and conditions of Rental: https://bit.ly/3Z99ps7
- Car Rental in Mozambique - Europcar: https://www.europcar.com/en/car-rental/locations/mozambique

2.6 Tour Companies

It may be easier to book tours to visit some of the attractions in Mozambique. Below are some recommended tour operators which can be used for tours in Mozambique.

- **Intrepid Travel**: Known for their adventurous and immersive tours, Intrepid Travel is another great option. Website: https://www.intrepidtravel.com/za/mozambique

- **Adventure to Africa**: They offer a variety of tours, including wildlife safaris and beach vacations. Website: https://www.adventuretoafrica.com/destinations/mozambique/

- **Giltedge Africa**: A luxury African safari and travel company, offering tailor-made trips to Mozambique. Website: https://giltedge.travel/destination/mozambique/

- **Extraordinary Journeys**: They offer unique and personalized safari experiences in Mozambique. Website: https://extraordinaryjourneys.com/destination/mozambique/

- **Somak Holidays**: They provide a wide range of holiday packages in Mozambique. Website: https://www.somak.com/mozambique

- **Travelo Mozambique**: A local travel agency that arranges custom tour packages with expert local tour guides. Website: https://www.travelomozambique.com/

- **Tours & Travel Mozambique**: A youthful Mozambican Travel Agent that shows the best of Mozambique, from the beaches to the wildlife. Website: https://www.africatouroperators.org/mozambique/mozambique-tour-operators/

Please note that it's always a good idea to check the latest reviews and verify the details from the official websites of these tour operators.

2.7 Other means of getting around

Below are some guidelines about other ways to get around Mozambique by walking and cycling.

Walking

Walking is a great way to explore the cities and towns of Mozambique. In particular, the capital city of Maputo is known for its wide avenues and colonial architecture, making it a pleasant city to explore on foot. However, like any city, it's important to stay aware of your surroundings, especially at night. Always ask your hotel or local contacts about the safety of the area before setting out.

Cycling and Quad Bike Rental

Cycling can be a fun and efficient way to get around, especially in some of the smaller towns or more touristy areas. Here are some places where you can rent a bike:

- o **Maputo Bike Rental**: They offer bike rentals in Maputo for four hours. You can collect the bike from a specified location. More Info: https://www.civitatis.com/en/maputo/bike-rental/

- o **Moz.Bike**: Located in Vilanculos, they offer various bike tours.

- o **Ilha Blue Island Safaris**: They offer bicycle hire on the Island of Mozambique. The island is flat and safe, perfect for biking. https://www.ilhablue.com/bicycle-hire

- o **Diversity Scuba**: In addition to scuba diving, they also offer quad bike rentals for more adventurous exploration. More Info: https://www.diversityscuba.com/kayaking

3 Where to stay in Mozambique

3.1 Districts in Mozambique

Mozambique is divided into several provinces and districts, each with its unique charm and attractions. Here are some of the key districts and suburbs that are suitable for first-time travellers.

Maputo
The capital city of Mozambique, Maputo, is a vibrant city with a mix of modern and colonial architecture. It's a great place to start your journey in Mozambique. The city is known for its lively markets, wide avenues, and a variety of restaurants and bars.

Matola
Located just outside of Maputo, Matola is the largest industrial area in Mozambique. It's a bustling city with a rich history and a variety of accommodation options.

Nampula
Nampula is the third-largest city in Mozambique and is known for its colonial architecture. It's a great base for exploring the nearby Mozambique Island, a UNESCO World Heritage Site.

Beira
Beira is the second-largest city in Mozambique and is a major port city. It's known for its beautiful beaches and the Beira Cathedral, a stunning example of Gothic architecture.

Quirimbas Archipelago
This is a chain of 32 coral islands stretching along the northern coast of Mozambique. It's a paradise for beach lovers and offers some of the best diving spots in the world. Medjumbe, Vamizi, and Matemo are known for being more isolated and remote, and for having pristine and nearly untouched beaches.

Tofo and Barra
These are beach resorts known for their white sandy beaches, bright blue waters, excellent diving, and friendly atmosphere. They are located just to the east of Inham

3.2 Hotels in Maputo, Mozambique

Here are some hotel options in Maputo, Mozambique that you might consider.

Radisson Blu Hotel & Residence, Maputo

- Star Rating: 5.0
- Guest Rating: 8.6 / 10.0
- Average Nightly Price: $202.74 (USD)
- Location: Located on the Strip, within 1 mi (2 km) of Núcleo de Arte, Museum of Natural History, and Vila Algarve. Geology Museum and Eduardo Mondlane University are also within 1 mi (2 km).
- Description: This family-friendly hotel offers a nearby beach, an onsite restaurant, and two bars/lounges.
- For more information and to make a booking visit the official website: https://www.radissonhotels.com/en-us/hotels/radisson-blu-maputo.

Southern Sun Maputo

- Star Rating: 4.0
- Guest Rating: 9.0 / 10.0
- Average Nightly Price: $197.41 (USD)
- Location: Nestled on the beach, this hotel is within 2 mi (3 km) of Eduardo Mondlane University, Fish Market, and Vila Algarve. Geology Museum and Núcleo de Arte are also within 3 mi (5 km).
- Description: This hotel features an outdoor pool, a restaurant, a fitness center, a bar/lounge, a 24-hour business center, and a conference center.
- For more information and to make a booking visit the official website: https://www.southernsun.com/southern-sun-maputo.

Polana Serena Hotel

- Star Rating: 4.5
- Guest Rating: 8.8 / 10.0
- Average Nightly Price: $199.15 (USD)
- Location: Situated within 1 mi (2 km) of Vila Algarve, Geology Museum, Núcleo de Arte, Museum of Natural History, and Shopping 24.
- Description: This luxury hotel has 3 restaurants, a full-service spa, an indoor pool, an outdoor pool, a fitness center, and a bar/lounge.
- For more information and to make a booking visit the official website: https://www.serenahotels.com/polana.

3.3 Hotels in Beira, Mozambique

Here are some hotels in Beira, Mozambique that you might find interesting.

Beira Terrace Hotel

- Star Rating: 4.0
- Average Nightly Price: $60.56 (USD)
- Location: situated in Beira, within a 10-minute walk of Casa Infante de Sagres and Praia Nova Market. Praca do Municipio and Beira Cathedral are also within 1 mi (2 km).
- Description: The hotel offers an outdoor pool, a restaurant, a fitness center, and a bar/lounge. Free buffet breakfast, free WiFi in public areas, and free self parking are also provided.
- For more information and to make a booking visit the official website: https://beira-terrace-hotel.booked.net/.

Hotel Tivoli Beira

- Star Rating: 3.0
- Average Nightly Price: $79.41 (USD)
- Location: Located in the heart of Beira, this 3-star hotel is within a 10-minute walk of Praia Nova Market, Praca do Municipio, and Casa Infante de Sagres. Beira Cathedral is 1 mi (1.5 km) away.
- Description: The hotel has a restaurant, a bar/lounge, and a coffee shop/cafe. Free WiFi in public areas and free self-parking are also provided
- For more information and to make a booking visit the official website: https://www.tdhotels.com/en/mozambique/hotels-beira/hotel-tivoli-beira/.

Golden Peacock Resort Hotel

- o Star Rating: 5.0
- o Average Nightly Price: $89.49 (USD)
- o Location: It is located 1.5 mi (2.4 km) from Makuti Lighthouse and 1.5 mi (2.5 km) from Beira Beach. Beira Cathedral and Praia Nova Market are also within 6 mi (10 km).
- o Description: The hotel offers an outdoor pool and a casino.
- o For more information and to make a booking visit the official website: https://www.hotelscombined.co.za/Hotel/Golden_Peacock_Resort_Hotel.htm

3.4 Hotels in Tofo and Barra

Here are some hotel options in Tofo and Barra for your consideration.

Eclectic Beach Retreat

- Location: Nestled on the beach, this Inhambane lodge is 0.1 mi (0.1 km) from Barra Beach and 9.9 mi (15.9 km) from Tofo Beach. Inhambane Park and Heroes' Square are also within 20 mi (32 km).
- Description: At Eclectic Beach Retreat, hit the beach, dine onsite at Onsite venue, or enjoy a drink at one of the lodge's 2 beach bars.
- Star Rating: 4.0
- Guest Rating: 10.0 / 10.0
- Average Nightly Price: $470.69 (USD)
- Book Here: https://eclecticbeachretreat.com/

Vertigo Lodge de Estuario

- Location: Situated near the airport, this lodge is 0.6 mi (1 km) from Tofo Beach and 5.1 mi (8.2 km) from Barra Beach. Heroes' Square and Market are also within 16 mi (25 km).
- Description: Along with an outdoor pool, this lodge has a restaurant and a bar/lounge. Free English breakfast, free WiFi in public areas, and free self parking are also provided. Other amenities include dry cleaning, laundry facilities, and tour/ticket assistance.
- Star Rating: 3.5
- Guest Rating: 10.0 / 10.0
- Average Nightly Price: $129.31 (USD)
- Book Here: https://vertigolodge.com/

Casa do Capitao

- Location: Situated near the airport, this hotel is within a 10-minute walk of Old Mosque, New Mosque, and New Cathedral. Inhambane Museum and Cathedral of Nossa Senhora de Conceição are also within 10 minutes.
- Description: Along with an outdoor pool, this smoke-free hotel has a restaurant and a bar/lounge. Free buffet breakfast is provided, as well as free WiFi in public areas, free self parking, and a free airport shuttle. Additionally, a snack bar/deli, a conference center, and laundry facilities are onsite.
- Star Rating: 4.0
- Guest Rating: 8.6 / 10.0
- Average Nightly Price: $151.40 (USD)
- Book Here: https://www.mozambique.co.za/Mozambique_Hotels_&_Resorts-travel/casa-do-capitao-inhambane.html

3.5 Food Culture of Mozambique

Mozambique's food culture is a vibrant blend of African, Portuguese, and other international influences, resulting in a cuisine that is rich, diverse, and full of flavor. Here are some of the must-try dishes and aspects of the food culture in Mozambique.

Seafood

Mozambique is renowned for its fresh seafood, with prawns being the most popular. They are often prepared with a spicy peri-peri sauce, a signature flavor of the region. Other seafood favorites include stonefish, clams, lobster, and crabs.

Galinha Asada

This is a traditional dish of grilled chicken, often marinated in peri-peri sauce. It's a staple in many Mozambican households and is also popular in restaurants.

Matapa Matapa is a traditional Mozambican dish made with cassava leaves, garlic, onion, and coconut milk, often served with rice. It can also include seafood or meat.

Chamussas

Chamussas are the Mozambican version of the Indian samosa, filled with meat or vegetables and deep-fried. They are a popular snack and can be found throughout the country.

Xima Xima, also known as 'pap', is a staple food in Mozambique. It's a type of cornmeal porridge and is often served with a sauce or stew.

Feijoada Feijoada is a hearty bean stew that is often made with beef and vegetables. It's a common dish in Mozambique and is often served with rice.

Meal Times
In Mozambique, breakfast is usually served early in the morning and can include tea or coffee, bread, and eggs. Lunch, the main meal of the day, is typically served from 12 pm to 2 pm and dinner is usually lighter and served in the evening. Snacks such as fresh fruit, nuts, and pastries are common throughout the day.

Languages
The official language of Mozambique is Portuguese, and many of the food terms will be in this language. However, English is also widely spoken, especially in tourist areas.

Remember, the food culture in Mozambique is diverse and varies by region, so don't be afraid to try new things and ask locals for their recommendations!

3.6 Traditional Food from Mozambique

Mozambique's traditional cuisine is a rich tapestry of flavors and influences, with a strong emphasis on fresh, local ingredients. The country's coastal location means that seafood plays a significant role in the diet, while maize, rice, and cassava form the staple carbohydrates. Here's a closer look at some of the traditional foods you might encounter in Mozambique, including those served during religious holidays.

Xima (Maize Porridge)
Xima, also known as 'pap', is a staple food in Mozambique. It's a type of cornmeal porridge and is often served with a sauce or stew. It's a common dish during both everyday meals and festive occasions.

Matapa
Matapa is a traditional Mozambican dish made with cassava leaves, garlic, onion, and coconut milk, often served with rice. It can also include seafood or meat. This dish is often served during special occasions and holidays.

Prawns
Mozambique is renowned for its fresh seafood, with prawns being the most popular. They are often prepared with a spicy peri-peri sauce, a signature flavor of the region. Prawns are a common feature during festive meals.

Galinha Asada
This is a traditional dish of grilled chicken, often marinated in peri-peri sauce. It's a staple in many Mozambican households and is also popular during religious holidays.

Bacalhão Bacalhão, or dried salted cod, is a traditional dish often served during religious holidays, particularly in the coastal regions of Mozambique.

Fresh Fruits Mozambique is rich in tropical fruits, and these often feature in festive meals. Fruits like mangoes, coconuts, and bananas are commonly used in desserts or eaten fresh.

During religious holidays, the food served often has symbolic significance. For example, during Christian holidays like Christmas and Easter, foods like chicken, goat, and special breads might be prepared. During Muslim holidays like Eid, special dishes like Biryani (a spiced rice dish) and sweet treats are often made.

It's important to note that the specific foods served can vary greatly depending on the region and the specific traditions of the community.

When visiting Mozambique, it's a wonderful experience to partake in these traditional meals and learn more about the cultural significance behind them.

3.7 Restaurants

Eating out in Mozambique is a must, and it is essential to try the seafood. Here are some of the best restaurants in Mozambique.

Casa Rex Restaurant
Located in Vilanculos, Casa Rex Restaurant is known for its seafood. The restaurant offers a variety of dishes, with an emphasis on fresh, locally sourced ingredients. The average cost per meal is around $15-$20.

Club Naval, Pemba
Club Naval in Pemba offers a Mediterranean menu with a Mozambican twist. The restaurant is known for its stunning views of the bay. The average cost per meal is around $20-$25.

Dhow Café
Dhow Café in Maputo is a popular spot for Greek cuisine. The restaurant is located in a beautiful setting with views of the ocean. The average cost per meal is around $15-$20.

Campo di Mare
Also located in Maputo, Campo di Mare is a great place for Italian cuisine. The restaurant is known for its pasta and seafood dishes. The average cost per meal is around $15-$20.

A Nossa Tasca
A Nossa Tasca in Maputo is a Portuguese restaurant that offers a variety of dishes, including seafood and meat dishes. The average cost per meal is around $10-$15.

Please note that prices can vary and it's always a good idea to check the restaurant's website or contact them directly for the most accurate information. Enjoy your culinary journey through Mozambique!

3.8 Markets

Below are some of the best markets and street food spots in Mozambique.

FEIMA - Feira de Artesanato, Flores e Gastronomica
Located in Maputo, FEIMA is a vibrant market that offers a wide variety of vendors selling everything from handicrafts to flowers. There are also two restaurants side by side, offering a taste of local cuisine. Bargaining is common here, so don't be shy to negotiate the prices.

Maputo Street Food
Street food in Maputo offers a unique taste of Mozambique's culinary culture. The food is minimally processed and offers a variety of homemade dishes.

YouTube Street Food Tour
For a visual tour of Mozambique's street food, you can check out this YouTube video) https://bit.ly/482IAtP . It provides a firsthand look at the street food culture in Mozambique.

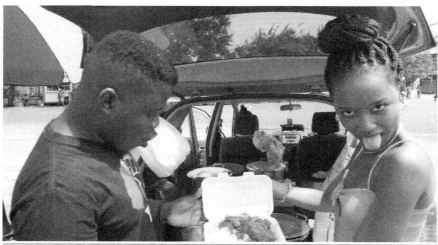

When visiting these markets and street food spots, it's important to remember a few things. First, always ensure that the food you're buying is freshly prepared and served hot to avoid any potential foodborne illnesses. Second, carry small denominations of the local currency for easier transactions. Lastly, embrace the experience!

Trying street food is a great way to immerse yourself in the local culture.

4 Top Attractions in Mozambique

4.1 Maputo, The Heart of Mozambique

Maputo, the capital city of Mozambique, is a bustling metropolis that beautifully blends African, Portuguese, and Arab cultures. It's a city that never sleeps, with a vibrant nightlife, rich history, and a plethora of attractions that cater to all types of travelers.

4.2 Historical Landmarks

Maputo is home to several historical landmarks that tell the story of the city's past. The **Maputo Central Train Station**, a majestic building designed by Gustave Eiffel, is a must-visit. The station still operates today and is considered one of the most beautiful railway stations in the world.

4.3 The Maputo Fortress

The Maputo Fortress, also known as Fortaleza da Nossa Senhora da Conceição, is another historical site worth visiting. This fortress was built in the late 18th century and played a crucial role in the city's defense during the colonial era.

4.4 Cultural Attractions

Maputo's cultural scene is as diverse as its history. The **National Art Museum** houses a significant collection of Mozambican art, including works by the renowned artist Malangatana Ngwenya.
The **Centro Cultural Franco-Moçambicano**, also known as the French-Mozambican Cultural Centre, is a hub for cultural activities, including concerts, exhibitions, and theater performances.

4.5 Natural Attractions

For nature lovers, **Inhaca Island** and the **Maputo Elephant Reserve** offer unforgettable experiences. Inhaca Island, a short boat ride from the city, is a paradise for snorkeling and bird watching. The Elephant Reserve, on the other hand, is home to elephants, hippos, and a variety of bird species.

4.6 Food and Markets

Maputo's food scene is a gastronomic delight. The **Fish Market**, or Mercado de Peixe, offers a wide range of fresh seafood that you can have cooked on the spot at nearby restaurants.

For shopping, the **FEIMA - Feira de Artesanato, Flores e Gastronomica** is a market where you can find handicrafts, flowers, and local cuisine.

Travel Tips

Maputo is generally safe for tourists, but like any city, it's important to stay vigilant, especially at night. Public transportation is available, but the most convenient way to get around is by taxi or car hire.

Most attractions in Maputo are open throughout the week, but it's always a good idea to check their official websites for the most accurate information.

4.7 Gorongosa National Park

Gorongosa National Park, located in the heart of central Mozambique, is often referred to as Africa's Greatest Conservation Story. The park is situated at the southern end of the Great African Rift Valley, a region known for its rich biodiversity and stunning landscapes.

The park was once one of Africa's finest wildlife destinations, teeming with a diverse array of animals and plants. However, the civil war in Mozambique led to its abandonment and a significant depletion of its wildlife. Despite these challenges, the park has experienced an incredible and inspiring rebirth, earning it the title of one of the "Last Wild Places" by National Geographic.

The restoration strategy for Gorongosa National Park is holistic, encompassing everything from advanced ecological and biological research to infrastructure development. This comprehensive approach has been instrumental in the park's recovery and continues to guide its management.

Today, visitors to Gorongosa National Park can witness its remarkable transformation firsthand. The park is home to a variety of wildlife, including elephants, lions, and a myriad of bird species. It also offers a range of activities for visitors, such as game drives, bird watching, and guided walks.

The park is open throughout the year, but the best time to visit is during the dry season, from April to October, when wildlife viewing is optimal. To get to Gorongosa National Park, you can take a flight to Beira or Maputo and then drive to the park. It's advisable to check the park's official website for the most up-to-date information on opening times and travel advisories.

Visiting Gorongosa National Park is not just about witnessing its natural beauty; it's also about understanding the importance of conservation and the role each one of us can play in preserving our planet's precious biodiversity.

For more information, please visit the official Gorongosa National Park website: https://gorongosa.org/.

4.8 Bazaruto Archipelago

The Bazaruto Archipelago is a group of six islands located in Mozambique, near the mainland city of Vilankulo. The archipelago is a true spectacle of nature, with its turquoise waters, sandy beaches, and diverse marine life. It is a paradise for nature lovers and adventure seekers alike.

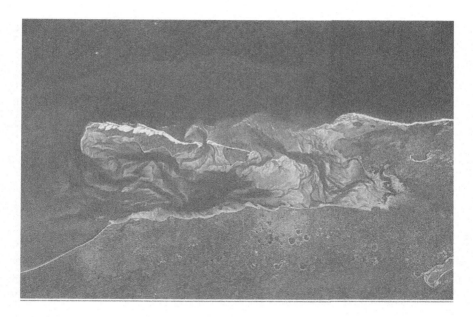

History

The islands of the Bazaruto Archipelago have a rich history that dates back centuries. The archipelago was once a part of a vast landmass that stretched from the Zambezi River to the Limpopo River. Over time, the sea level rose, and the landmass was submerged, leaving only the highest sand dunes visible above the water. These dunes eventually became the islands of the Bazaruto Archipelago.

Interesting Facts

The Bazaruto Archipelago is home to over 140 bird species, making it a bird watcher's paradise. The pristine waters surrounding the islands are teeming with colourful fish and other marine life, offering excellent opportunities for diving and snorkelling. The archipelago was declared a National Park in 1971, further cementing its status as a haven for wildlife.

Visiting the Bazaruto Archipelago

The Bazaruto Archipelago is accessible via boat or plane from the mainland city of Vilankulo. There are several resorts on the islands that offer accommodation for visitors. These resorts often provide activities such as diving, snorkelling, bird watching, and fishing.

The best time to visit the Bazaruto Archipelago is during the dry season, which runs from April to November. During this time, the weather is pleasant, and the sea conditions are ideal for water-based activities.

Opening Times
The Bazaruto Archipelago is open to visitors all year round. However, it is advisable to check with your travel agent or the resort you are staying at for any changes in visiting hours or restrictions due to weather conditions or other factors.

Please note that it's always recommended to check the latest travel advisories and local regulations before planning your visit to any foreign destination. Enjoy your visit to the beautiful Bazaruto Archipelago!

4.9   Ilha de Mozambique: A Historical Gem

Overview
Ilha de Mozambique is a captivating UNESCO World Heritage Site located off the northern coast of Mozambique in Africa. This small coral island, spanning just 3 km in length and less than half a kilometer in width, is steeped in history and brimming with architectural treasures. It served as the capital of Mozambique for nearly four centuries under Portuguese rule and was a major Arab

port long before that. The island is a melting pot of cultural influences, with a blend of African, Arab, and European heritage.

Historical Significance
The island's historical significance is evident in its diverse architectural styles. The northern Stone Town is home to old colonial buildings, including the impressive St. Sebastian Fortress built in the 16th century, and the Chapel of Nossa Senhora de Baluarte, which is considered to be the oldest European building in the southern hemisphere. The southern part, known as Reed Town, features traditional Mozambican houses made of reeds.

Interesting Facts
One of the most iconic landmarks on the island is the Palace and Chapel of São Paulo, built in 1610 as a Jesuit College and later converted into a palace. Today, it houses a fascinating museum showcasing the island's history. Another interesting fact is that the island was a major hub for the gold, ivory, and slave trade during the 17th and 18th centuries.

Visiting Tips

When visiting Ilha de Mozambique, it's recommended to take a guided tour to fully appreciate the historical context of the sites. The island is small enough to explore on foot, but you can also hire a bicycle or take a tuk-tuk. Don't miss the opportunity to sample local cuisine, which reflects the island's cultural mix, with seafood being a specialty.

Location and How to Get There

Ilha de Mozambique is located in Nampula Province, Northern Mozambique. The nearest airport is in Nampula city, which is about 180 km from the island. From Nampula, you can take a taxi or a bus to the island. If you're coming from the capital, Maputo, you can take a domestic flight to Nampula.

Opening Times

Most of the historical sites and museums on the island are open from 8:30 am to 5:30 pm, but it's always a good idea to check the specific opening times of each place you plan to visit.

Visiting Ilha de Mozambique is like stepping back in time. Its rich history, unique architecture, and vibrant local culture make it a must-visit destination for any traveler to Mozambique.

4.10 Inhambane: A Coastal Paradise

Overview
Inhambane is a charming city located in southern Mozambique, known for its serene beaches, historic colonial architecture, and vibrant local culture. It is one of the oldest settlements on the East Coast of Africa and has a rich history dating back to the 11th century.

Historical Significance
Inhambane was a key trading post in the Indian Ocean, known for its trade in ivory and slaves. The city's name is derived from the word "Inhambane," which means "the place of the friendly people" in the local language. The city's historical significance is evident in its well-preserved colonial architecture, including the 18th-century Cathedral of Our Lady of Conception, which offers panoramic views of the city from its rusted iron ladder.

Interesting Facts
Inhambane is known for its traditional dhows (sailing vessels), which are still used by local fishermen. The city is also famous for its nearby beaches, such as Tofo Beach, known for its excellent surfing, diving, and abundant marine life, including manta rays and whale sharks.

Visiting Tips
When visiting Inhambane, make sure to explore both the city and its surrounding beaches. The city's central market is a great place to experience local life and buy fresh produce and local handicrafts. For those interested in marine life, a trip to Tofo Beach for a diving or snorkeling excursion is a must. Don't miss the opportunity to sample local cuisine, especially the seafood, which is fresh and plentiful.

Location and How to Get There
Inhambane is located in southern Mozambique, about 470 km northeast of the capital, Maputo. The city has its own airport, Inhambane Airport, with regular flights from Maputo and Johannesburg, South Africa. Alternatively, you can take a bus or drive from Maputo, which takes about 6-7 hours.

Opening Times
Inhambane is a city, so it doesn't have specific opening times. However, most businesses and attractions operate from around 8:00 am to 5:00 pm. It's always a good idea to check the specific opening times of each place you plan to visit.

Inhambane offers a unique blend of history, culture, and natural beauty, making it a must-visit destination for any traveler to Mozambique. Whether you're exploring the city's historic streets, relaxing on its pristine beaches, or diving in its crystal-clear waters, you're sure to fall in love with Inhambane.

4.11 Pemba: A Tropical Haven

Overview
Pemba is a picturesque port city located in northern Mozambique, known for its beautiful beaches, clear turquoise waters, and vibrant local culture. It is the gateway to the Quirimbas Archipelago, a chain of 32 coral islands stretching up the coast and is renowned for its Portuguese colonial architecture.

Historical Significance
Founded in 1904 as Porto Amelia, after the queen of Portugal, Pemba has a rich history as a trading port. It was a key port for the Portuguese, dealing in spices, gold, and slaves. Today, it's known for

its trade in traditional silverware and Makonde wood carvings, a craft of the Makonde people native to the region.

Interesting Facts
Pemba is known for its natural beauty, particularly its coral reefs which are a haven for divers and snorkelers. The city is also famous for its Baobab trees, some of which are hundreds of years old. Pemba Bay, one of the world's largest natural harbors, is a sight to behold.

Visiting Tips
When visiting Pemba, make sure to explore both the city and its surrounding natural attractions. The city's bustling market, Mercado Central, is a great place to experience local life and buy fresh produce, local handicrafts, and traditional silverware. A trip to the Quirimbas Archipelago is a must for its pristine beaches and excellent diving and snorkeling opportunities. Don't miss the opportunity to sample local cuisine, particularly the seafood, which is fresh and plentiful.

Location and How to Get There
Pemba is located in northern Mozambique, about 1700 km north of the capital, Maputo. The city has its own airport, Pemba Airport, with regular flights from Maputo and Johannesburg, South Africa. Alternatively, you can take a bus or drive from Maputo, but be prepared for a long journey.

Opening Times
Pemba is a city, so it doesn't have specific opening times. However, most businesses and attractions operate from around 8:00 am to 5:00 pm. It's always a good idea to check the specific opening times of each place you plan to visit.

Pemba offers a unique blend of history, culture, and natural beauty, making it a must-visit destination for any traveler to Mozambique. Whether you're exploring the city's historic streets, relaxing on its pristine beaches, or diving in its crystal-clear waters, you're sure to fall in love with Pemba.

4.12 Niassa Reserve: A Wildlife Wonderland

Overview

The Niassa Reserve is one of Africa's last true wilderness areas. Located in northern Mozambique, this vast natural reserve spans over 42,000 square kilometers, making it the largest protected area in the country. It is roughly twice the size of South Africa's famous Kruger National Park.

Historical Significance
Established in 1954, the Niassa Reserve has a rich history of conservation. Despite challenges during Mozambique's civil war, the reserve has rebounded and is now a beacon of biodiversity. It is home to significant populations of African wildlife, including elephants, lions, leopards, and African wild dogs. The reserve is also known for its unique Miombo woodland ecosystems and is a critical sanctuary for the threatened African elephant.

Interesting Facts
One of the most fascinating aspects of the Niassa Reserve is its biodiversity. It is home to over 400 bird species and more than 200 mammal species. The reserve also boasts one of the largest and most viable African wild dog populations in the world. Additionally, Niassa is recognized for its cultural significance, with over 40,000 people from various ethnic groups living within its boundaries.

Visiting Tips
Visiting the Niassa Reserve is a true adventure. Game drives and walking safaris are the best ways to explore the reserve and see its wildlife up close. Birdwatching is also a popular activity given the reserve's diverse birdlife. When visiting, it's important to respect the reserve's rules and guidelines to ensure the safety and preservation of its wildlife.

Location and How to Get There
The Niassa Reserve is located in northern Mozambique, bordering Tanzania. The best way to reach the reserve is by charter flight from Pemba or Nampula, which are the nearest cities with airports. There are several camps and lodges within the reserve that can arrange these flights.

Opening Times
The Niassa Reserve is open year-round, but the best time to visit is during the dry season, from June to October, when wildlife viewing is

optimal. It's always a good idea to check with your accommodation for specific visiting hours and any potential closures.

The Niassa Reserve offers a unique and off-the-beaten-path safari experience. Its vast landscapes, abundant wildlife, and cultural richness make it a must-visit destination for any nature and wildlife enthusiast.

4.13 Quirimbas Archipelago: A Tropical Paradise

Overview

The Quirimbas Archipelago is a string of 32 stunning coral islands stretching along the northern coast of Mozambique in the Indian Ocean. Known for their breathtaking beauty, these islands offer pristine white sandy beaches, crystal clear waters, and abundant marine life, making them a paradise for beach lovers, divers, and snorkelers.

Historical Significance

The Quirimbas Archipelago has a rich and diverse history. The islands were a key trading post from the 10th to the 16th century, first with Arab merchants and later with the Portuguese. The archipelago was known for its trade in gold, ivory, and slaves. Many of the islands have remnants of Portuguese colonial architecture, including the fortresses on Ibo Island, which is now a UNESCO World Heritage Site.

Interesting Facts

The Quirimbas Archipelago is home to the Quirimbas National Park, which encompasses 11 of the southernmost islands. The park is known for its diverse ecosystems, including mangroves, coral reefs, and rainforests, and is home to a variety of wildlife, such as elephants, lions, and leopards. The archipelago is also a nesting ground for sea turtles.

Visiting Tips

When visiting the Quirimbas Archipelago, make sure to take advantage of the excellent diving and snorkeling opportunities. The archipelago is known for its diverse and vibrant coral reefs, which are home to a variety of marine life, including dolphins, turtles, and a multitude of tropical fish. Don't miss the opportunity to explore the historical sites on Ibo Island. When planning your visit, consider staying in one of the many luxury lodges or resorts that offer a range of activities, from dhow sailing trips to cultural tours.

Location and How to Get There
The Quirimbas Archipelago is located off the northern coast of Mozambique. The nearest city with an airport is Pemba, which has regular flights from Maputo and Johannesburg, South Africa. From Pemba, you can take a charter flight or a boat to the islands.

Opening Times
The Quirimbas Archipelago can be visited year-round, but the best time to visit is during the dry season, from May to November, when the weather is most favorable. It's always a good idea to check with your accommodation for specific visiting hours and any potential closures.

The Quirimbas Archipelago offers a unique blend of natural beauty, rich history, and cultural diversity, making it a must-visit destination for any traveler to Mozambique. Whether you're exploring the coral reefs, relaxing on the beaches, or discovering the islands' history, you're sure to have an unforgettable experience.

4.14 Chimanimani Mountains: A Hiker's Paradise

Overview
The Chimanimani Mountains are a range of mountains that straddle the border between Zimbabwe and Mozambique. Known for their rugged beauty and diverse flora and fauna, these mountains are a paradise for hikers, nature lovers, and bird watchers.

Historical Significance
The Chimanimani Mountains have been inhabited for thousands of years, with evidence of early human settlement found in the form of rock paintings in the region. The mountains were traditionally considered a sacred place by the local communities. Today, they are part of the larger Chimanimani Transfrontier Park, a conservation area that spans the border between Zimbabwe and Mozambique.

Interesting Facts
The Chimanimani Mountains are known for their unique biodiversity. They are home to several endemic species of plants and animals, including the rare Chimanimani frog. The mountains also boast stunning natural features, such as the Bridal Veil Falls, a 50-meter waterfall located near the town of Chimanimani.

Visiting Tips

When visiting the Chimanimani Mountains, be prepared for some challenging but rewarding hikes. The mountains offer a range of trails for all levels of fitness and experience. Make sure to bring sturdy hiking shoes, plenty of water, and sun protection. Bird watchers should bring binoculars, as the region is home to a variety of bird species. For accommodation, there are several campsites and lodges in and around the town of Chimanimani.

Location and How to Get There

The Chimanimani Mountains are located in eastern Zimbabwe, near the border with Mozambique. The nearest city with an airport is Harare, the capital of Zimbabwe. From Harare, you can take a bus or drive to the town of Chimanimani, which is the gateway to the mountains. The journey from Harare to Chimanimani takes about 5-6 hours by road.

Opening Times

The Chimanimani Mountains can be visited year-round, but the best time to visit is during the dry season, from April to October, when the weather is most favorable for hiking. It's always a good idea to check with local authorities or your accommodation for specific visiting hours and any potential closures.

The Chimanimani Mountains offer a unique blend of natural beauty, rich history, and biodiversity, making them a must-visit destination for any traveler to Zimbabwe or Mozambique. Whether you're hiking the rugged trails, spotting wildlife, or simply soaking in the stunning views, you're sure to have an unforgettable experience.

4.15 Swimming with Dolphins

There are many tailor-made tours for Mozambique. One of the most unique experiences is to swim with dolphins at Ponto do Ouro. This is an unforgettable experience to interact with these gentle creatures. For more information please visit The Dolphin Centre website at https://thedolphincentre.com/.

5 Culture and Entertainment in Mozambique

5.1 Art Galleries

Núcleo de Arte
Located in the capital city of Maputo, the Núcleo de Arte is one of the most important contemporary art galleries in Mozambique. It's a vibrant art space that houses a diverse collection of works from Mozambican artists, including paintings, sculptures, and ceramics. The gallery also hosts regular exhibitions and workshops.
Location: R. da Argélia 194, Maputo, Mozambique
Opening Times: Generally, Monday to Friday from 9:00 am to 5:00 pm, and Saturday from 9:00 am to 1:00 pm. However, it's recommended to check before visiting.
Entrance Fee: Free

Kulungwana Espaço Artístico
Kulungwana Espaço Artístico is another notable art gallery located in Maputo. The gallery is situated in the Central Railway Station, a historic building known for its architectural beauty. Kulungwana hosts a variety of exhibitions showcasing the works of both established and emerging Mozambican artists.
Location: Praca dos Trabalhadores, Maputo, Mozambique *Opening Times*: Usually open from Monday to Friday, 9:00 am to 5:00 pm. It's advisable to check the exact timings before your visit.
Entrance Fee: Free

Machilla Magic
Machilla Magic is an art gallery and craft center located in the coastal town of Vilankulo. The gallery showcases a wide range of arts and crafts made by local artists and craftsmen, including sculptures, paintings, textiles, and jewelry.
Location: Vilankulo, Inhambane Province, Mozambique *Opening Times*: Typically open daily from 8:00 am to 5:00 pm. It's recommended to confirm the timings before your visit.
Entrance Fee: Free

Please note that the opening times and entrance fees are subject to change, and it's always a good idea to check with the galleries directly for the most accurate and up-to-date information.

5.2 Museums

Museu de História Natural (Natural History Museum)
Located in the capital city of Maputo, the Museu de História Natural is one of the most visited museums in Mozambique. It houses a vast collection of Mozambique's flora and fauna, including preserved specimens of the country's wildlife. One of the museum's highlights is its collection of elephant fetuses, which is believed to be unique in the world.

Location: Praça Travessia do Zambeze, Maputo, Mozambique
Opening Times: Generally, Tuesday to Sunday from 9:00 am to 5:00 pm. However, it's recommended to check before visiting.
Entrance Fee: There may be a small entrance fee, but it's best to check with the museum for the most accurate information.

Museu Nacional de Arte (National Art Museum)
The Museu Nacional de Arte in Maputo is a must-visit for art lovers. It showcases a wide range of artworks from Mozambican artists, including paintings, sculptures, and drawings. The museum regularly hosts temporary exhibitions, offering visitors a chance to experience the vibrant and dynamic art scene of Mozambique.

Location: Av. Ho Chi Minh 1238, Maputo, Mozambique
Opening Times: Usually open from Monday to Friday, 9:00 am to 5:00 pm, and Saturday from 9:00 am to 1:00 pm. It's advisable to check the exact timings before your visit.
Entrance Fee: There may be a small entrance fee, but it's best to check with the museum for the most accurate information.

Museu da Moeda (Currency Museum)
The Museu da Moeda, also located in Maputo, offers a fascinating look into the economic history of Mozambique. The museum displays a collection of currency used in Mozambique from pre-colonial times to the present day. It's housed in a historic building that was once the Bank of Mozambique.

Location: Av. 25 de Setembro 1695, Maputo, Mozambique *Opening Times*: Typically open from Monday to Friday, 9:00 am to 4:00 pm. It's recommended to confirm the timings before your visit.
Entrance Fee: Free

5.3 Theatres

Here is some general information about a few well-known theatres in Mozambique.

Teatro Avenida
Located in the capital city of Maputo, the Teatro Avenida is one of the most important cultural venues in Mozambique. It hosts a variety of performances, including plays, concerts, dance performances, and film screenings. The theatre is known for its beautiful architecture and its commitment to promoting Mozambican culture and arts.
Location: Avenida Karl Marx, Maputo, Mozambique
Types of Shows: Plays, concerts, dance performances, film screenings
Ticket Prices: Prices vary depending on the event, but it's best to check with the theatre for the most accurate information.

Centro Cultural Franco-Moçambicano (CCFM)
The Centro Cultural Franco-Moçambicano, also located in Maputo, is a cultural center that includes a theatre. The CCFM hosts a wide range of events, including theatre performances, concerts, exhibitions, and workshops. It's a vibrant hub of cultural activity and a great place to experience the arts scene in Mozambique.
Location: Avenida Samora Machel, Maputo, Mozambique *Types of Shows*: Theatre performances, concerts, exhibitions, workshops
Ticket Prices: Prices vary depending on the event, but it's best to check with the centre for the most accurate information.
Please note that the information about types of shows and ticket prices is subject to change, and it's always a good idea to check with the theatres directly for the most accurate and up-to-date information.

5.4 Nightlife in Mozambique

Maputo Nightlife
Maputo, the capital city of Mozambique, is known for its vibrant nightlife. The city is home to a variety of bars, clubs, and restaurants that come alive after dark.

Coconuts Live

This is one of the most popular nightclubs in Maputo. It offers a mix of local and international music and is known for its lively atmosphere.
Location: Avenida Marginal, Maputo, Mozambique

Gil Vicente
This is a combination of a bar, café, and live music venue. It's a great place to experience local music and culture.
Location: Avenida Samora Machel, Maputo, Mozambique

Tofo Nightlife
Tofo, a beach town in Inhambane Province, is another great place to experience Mozambique's nightlife. The town is known for its beach bars and relaxed vibe.

Dino's Beach Bar
This beachfront bar is a popular spot for both locals and tourists. It offers a variety of drinks and often has live music.
Location: Praia do Tofo, Tofo, Mozambique

Pemba Nightlife
Pemba, in northern Mozambique, also offers a range of nightlife options. The city has several bars and restaurants where you can enjoy a night out.

Pemba Beach Hotel & Spa
While it's a hotel, it's also known for its bars and restaurants. It's a great place to enjoy a drink while overlooking the ocean.
Location: Avenida da Marginal, Pemba, Mozambique
Please note that the opening times and offerings of these venues may vary, and it's always a good idea to check with them directly for the most accurate and up-to-date information.

5.5   Shopping in Mozambique

Below is some general information about shopping in Mozambique.

Mercado Central de Maputo
Located in the capital city of Maputo, the Mercado Central de Maputo is a bustling market where you can find a wide variety of goods. From fresh produce and seafood to crafts and textiles, this market offers a glimpse into the daily life of locals in Maputo.

Location: Avenida 25 de Setembro, Maputo, Mozambique
Type of Shopping: Fresh produce, seafood, crafts, textiles

Feima - Feira de Artesanato, Flores e Gastronomica

Feima is a craft fair located in Maputo. Here, you can find a wide range of Mozambican handicrafts, including wood carvings, paintings, ceramics, and textiles. It's a great place to buy souvenirs and gifts.
Location: Parque dos Continuadores, Maputo, Mozambique
Type of Shopping: Handicrafts, souvenirs

Shopping 24

Shopping 24 is a modern shopping mall located in Maputo. It offers a variety of shops, including clothing stores, electronics shops, and supermarkets. There are also several restaurants and cafes where you can take a break from shopping.
Location: Avenida Julius Nyerere, Maputo, Mozambique
Type of Shopping: Clothing, electronics, groceries

Machilla Magic

Located in the coastal town of Vilankulo, *Machilla Magic* is an art gallery and craft center where you can buy a wide range of arts and crafts made by local artists and craftsmen, including sculptures, paintings, textiles, and jewelry.
Location: Vilankulo, Inhambane Province, Mozambique
Type of Shopping: Arts and crafts.

Please note that the opening times and offerings of these venues may vary, and it's always a good idea to check with them directly for the most accurate and up-to-date information.

6   Day Trips and Excursions

6.1   One Day tour of Maputo

08:00 - Breakfast
Start your day with a hearty breakfast at your hotel or one of the many restaurants in Maputo.

09:00 - Visit the Fortress of Maputo
After breakfast, head to the Fortress of Maputo, also known as Fortaleza de Nossa Senhora da Conceição. This historical site offers a glimpse into Mozambique's colonial past. Inside, you'll find a museum displaying various historical artifacts.
Location: Praça 25 de Junho, Maputo, Mozambique
Website: No official website, but you can find information on various travel sites.
Price: Free entry *Tip*: Hire a local guide at the entrance to learn more about the history of the fortress.

10:30 - Explore the Central Market
Next, visit the Central Market, also known as Mercado Central de Maputo. Here, you can find a wide variety of goods, from fresh produce and seafood to crafts and textiles. It's a great place to experience the local culture and maybe pick up a few souvenirs.
Location: Avenida 25 de Setembro, Maputo, Mozambique
Price: Free entry but bring some cash if you plan to buy anything.

12:00 - Lunch at Piri Piri
For lunch, head to Piri Piri, a popular restaurant known for its delicious Mozambican cuisine. Try their signature dish, the piri piri chicken, a spicy grilled chicken dish that's a local favorite.
Location: Avenida Martires de Mueda, Maputo, Mozambique *Website*: Unfortunately, they do not have a website, but you can check their reviews on TripAdvisor.
Price: Expect to spend around MZN 500-700 for lunch.

14:00 - Visit the Natural History Museum
After lunch, visit the Natural History Museum, also known as Museu de História Natural. The museum has a large collection of taxidermy animals, fossils, and anthropological exhibits.

Location: Praça Travessia do Zambeze, Maputo, Mozambique
Website: No official website, but you can find information on various travel sites.
Price: MZN 50 for entry
Tip: The museum's elephant fetus exhibit is one of its most famous displays.

16:00 - Stroll along Avenida Julius Nyerere

Spend the late afternoon strolling along Avenida Julius Nyerere, one of the main streets in Maputo. The avenue is lined with shops, cafes, and beautiful colonial-era buildings.

18:00 - Dinner at Campo di Mare

For dinner, head to Campo di Mare, an Italian restaurant with a Mozambican twist. The restaurant is located by the sea, offering beautiful views as you dine.
Location: Avenida Marginal, Maputo, Mozambique
Website: Unfortunately, they do not have a website, but you can check their reviews on TripAdvisor.
Price: Expect to spend around MZN 800-1000 for dinner.

20:00 - Enjoy the Nightlife at Coconuts Live

End your day by experiencing Maputo's vibrant nightlife at *Coconuts Live*, one of the city's most popular nightclubs. Enjoy a mix of local and international music and dance the night away.
Location: Avenida Marginal, Maputo, Mozambique
Website: Unfortunately, they do not have a website, but you can check their reviews on TripAdvisor.
Price: Entry fees vary depending on the event but expect to spend around MZN 500-1000.

23:00 - End of the Day

After a night of dancing, it's time to head back to your accommodation and rest up for your next day of adventures in Mozambique.

Please note that the times, prices, and locations mentioned are subject to change and it's always a good idea to check with the venues directly for the most accurate and up-to-date information. Also, moving from one place to another in Maputo can be done by taxi or tuk-tuk, and most journeys within the city should take no more than 20-30 minutes.

6.1.1 Map of One Day Tour of Maputo

Interactive link to the map: https://bit.ly/3PaV89M

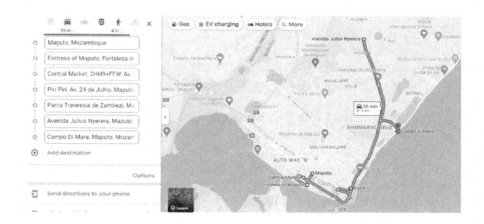

6.2 One-day Beach Escape in Tofo

08:00 - Breakfast at Branko's
Start your day with a hearty breakfast at Branko's, a popular spot in Tofo known for its delicious food and great coffee. Try their fresh fruit and granola, or if you're in the mood for something more substantial, their full English breakfast is highly recommended.
Location: Praia do Tofo, Inhambane, Mozambique
Price: Expect to spend around MZN 200-300 for breakfast.

09:00 - Morning Beach Walk
After breakfast, take a leisurely walk along Tofo Beach. The beach is known for its soft white sand and clear turquoise waters. It's a great place to relax and soak in the beauty of the Mozambican coastline.
Location: Praia do Tofo, Inhambane, Mozambique
Price: Free

10:00 - Visit the Marine Megafauna Foundation
Next, visit the Marine Megafauna Foundation, a research and conservation organization dedicated to protecting marine life. They offer educational talks about the local marine ecosystem and the species that inhabit it, including manta rays and whale sharks.
Location: Praia do Tofo, Inhambane, Mozambique

Website: Marine Megafauna Foundation:
https://marinemegafaunafoundation.org/
Price: Donations are appreciated.

12:00 - Lunch at Casa de Comer

For lunch, head to Casa de Comer, a restaurant known for its delicious seafood. Try their grilled calamari or the seafood platter, which includes prawns, calamari, and fish.
Location: Praia do Tofo, Inhambane, Mozambique
Price: Expect to spend around MZN 500-700 for lunch.

14:00 - Snorkeling or Diving with Tofo Scuba

After lunch, it's time for some adventure. Tofo Scuba offers snorkeling and diving trips where you can see a variety of marine life, including manta rays, dolphins, and even whale sharks if you're lucky.
Location: Praia do Tofo, Inhambane, Mozambique
Website: Tofo Scuba: http://www.tofoscuba.com/
Price: Prices vary depending on the activity, but expect to spend around MZN 2000-3000.

18:00 - Sunset at Dino's Beach Bar

After a day of adventure, relax and enjoy the sunset at *Dino's Beach Bar*. This beachfront bar is the perfect place to unwind with a drink and enjoy the stunning views of the Indian Ocean.
Location: Praia do Tofo, Inhambane, Mozambique
Price: Drinks range from MZN 100-200.

20:00 - Dinner at What U Want

End your day with a delicious dinner at What U Want, a popular restaurant in Tofo. They offer a variety of dishes, but their pizza is a must-try.
Location: Praia do Tofo, Inhambane, Mozambique
Price: Expect to spend around MZN 500-700 for dinner.

22:00 - Nightlife at Mozambeat Motel

If you're up for some nightlife, head to the Mozambeat Motel. They often have live music or DJs, and it's a great place to meet other travelers and dance the night away.
Location: Praia do Tofo, Inhambane, Mozambique
Website: Mozambeat Motel : https://www.mozambeatmotel.com/
Price: Entry is free, drinks range from MZN 100-200.

23:00 - End of the Day
After a night of fun, it's time to head back to your accommodation and rest up for your next day of adventures in Mozambique.

Please note that the times, prices, and locations mentioned are subject to change and it's always a good idea to check with the venues directly for the most accurate and up-to-date information.

Moving from one place to another in Tofo can be done by foot as the town is quite small and everything is within walking distance.

6.2.1   Map to the One-day Beach Escape to Tofu

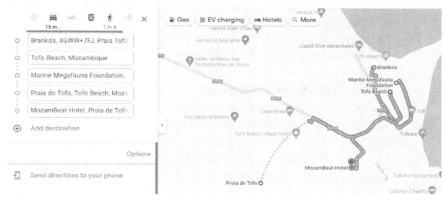

6.3   One-day Wildlife Adventure in Gorongosa National Park
08:00 - Breakfast at Your Accommodation
Start your day with a hearty breakfast at your accommodation. You'll need plenty of energy for the day ahead!

09:00 - Arrival at Gorongosa National Park
Arrive at Gorongosa National Park, one of the most biodiverse places on the planet. The park is home to a wide variety of wildlife, including elephants, lions, and over 500 species of birds.
Location: Sofala Province, Mozambique
Website: Gorongosa National Park
Price: Entry fee is $20 per person.

10:00 - Morning Game Drive

Embark on a morning game drive through the park. This is a great time to spot wildlife as many animals are most active during the cooler morning hours. Keep your eyes peeled for lions, elephants, and a variety of antelope species.

Location: Gorongosa National Park, Sofala Province, Mozambique
Price: Game drives are included with the park entry fee.

13:00 - Picnic Lunch

Enjoy a picnic lunch in the park. Many accommodations can prepare a packed lunch for you, or you can bring your own food and drinks. Remember to leave no trace and keep a safe distance from wildlife.

14:00 - Visit the Community Education Center

After lunch, visit the Community Education Center to learn about the park's conservation efforts and the role of local communities in preserving this unique ecosystem.

Location: Gorongosa National Park, Sofala Province, Mozambique
Price: Included with the park entry fee.

15:00 - Afternoon Game Drive

Embark on an afternoon game drive. This is another great opportunity to spot wildlife, including predators that may start to become more active as the day cools down.

Location: Gorongosa National Park, Sofala Province, Mozambique
Price: Game drives are included with the park entry fee.

18:00 - Sunset at the Park

Enjoy a stunning sunset in the park. This is a magical time of day in Gorongosa, with beautiful light and active wildlife.

19:00 - Return to Your Accommodation

Return to your accommodation for dinner and a well-deserved rest after a full day of wildlife viewing.

23:00 - End of the Day

Time for a good night's sleep to recharge for your next day of adventures in Mozambique!

Also, keep in mind that Gorongosa National Park is a large area and travel times between different parts of the park can vary. Always allow plenty of time to get from one place to another.

6.3.1 Map from Maputo to Gorongosa National Park

Interactive link to the map: https://bit.ly/3Rj5cQG

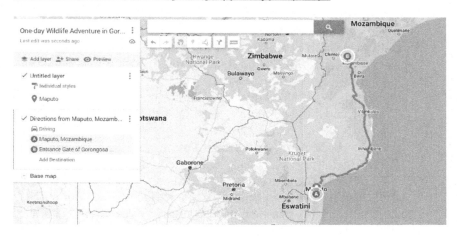

6.4 One-day Historical Journey in Ilha de Mozambique

08:00 - Breakfast at Your Accommodation
Start your day with a hearty breakfast at your accommodation. You'll need plenty of energy for the day ahead!

09:00 - Arrival at Ilha de Mozambique
Arrive at Ilha de Mozambique, a UNESCO World Heritage Site known for its unique blend of cultural influences and well-preserved colonial architecture.
Location: Nampula Province, Mozambique

10:00 - Visit the Palace of São Paulo
Begin your historical journey at the Palace of São Paulo, a former governor's residence that now houses the Museum of Sacred Art. Here, you can see a collection of religious artifacts and enjoy panoramic views of the island from the upper floors.
Location: Ilha de Mozambique, Nampula Province, Mozambique
Website: Museum of Sacred Art:
http://www.mozambiqueisland.com/
Price: Entry fee is around MZN 200 per person.

11:30 - Explore the Fort of São Sebastião

Next, visit the Fort of São Sebastião, the oldest complete fort still standing in sub-Saharan Africa. The fort also houses the Chapel of Nossa Senhora de Baluarte, considered to be the oldest European building in the southern hemisphere.
Location: Ilha de Mozambique, Nampula Province, Mozambique
Price: Entry fee is around MZN 200 per person.

13:00 - Lunch at Karibu Restaurant
For lunch, head to Karibu Restaurant, known for its delicious seafood and great views of the ocean.
Location: Ilha de Mozambique, Nampula Province, Mozambique
Price: Expect to spend around MZN 500-700 for lunch.

14:30 - Walk Along the Stone Town
After lunch, take a leisurely walk through the Stone Town, the oldest part of Ilha de Mozambique. The area is known for its narrow streets and colonial-era buildings with beautifully carved doors.
Location: Ilha de Mozambique, Nampula Province, Mozambique
Price: Free

16:00 - Visit the Maritime Museum
Next, visit the Maritime Museum, which showcases the island's rich maritime history. The museum houses a collection of artifacts from shipwrecks found around the island.
Location: Ilha de Mozambique, Nampula Province, Mozambique
Price: Entry fee is around MZN 200 per person.

18:00 - Enjoy the Sunset at the Beach
End your day by enjoying a beautiful sunset at the beach. The beaches of Ilha de Mozambique are known for their clear waters and stunning views of the Indian Ocean.
Location: Ilha de Mozambique, Nampula Province, Mozambique
Price: Free

19:30 - Dinner at Reliquias Restaurant
For dinner, head to Reliquias Restaurant, a popular spot known for its Mozambican and Portuguese cuisine.
Location: Ilha de Mozambique, Nampula Province, Mozambique
Price: Expect to spend around MZN 500-700 for dinner.

21:00 - Stroll Through the Market

After dinner, take a stroll through the local market. It's a great place to buy souvenirs and experience the local culture.
Location: Ilha de Mozambique, Nampula Province, Mozambique
Price: Prices vary depending on what you buy.

23:00 - End of the Day
Return to your accommodation for a well-deserved rest after a full day of exploring Ilha de Mozambique.

Please note that the times, prices, and locations mentioned are subject to change and it's always a good idea to check with the venues directly for the most accurate and up-to-date information. Also, keep in mind that Ilha de Mozambique is a small island, and most places are within walking distance.

6.4.1   One-day Historical Journey in Ilha de Mozambique

Interactive link to the map: https://bit.ly/45EUU1W

6.5   From Maputo: Day trip to Ponta do Oura

Take a day trip to one of the most beautiful bays on the Mozambican coast. Enjoy the pristine blue waters and white sands of Ponta de Ouro on a day trip from Maputo. The price starts at US$ 250 per person.

08:00 - Breakfast at Your Accommodation
Start your day with a hearty breakfast at your accommodation in Maputo. You'll need plenty of energy for the day ahead!
09:00 - Departure from Maputo

Depart from Maputo for Ponta do Ouro, a charming beach town located near the South African border. The drive takes about 2.5 hours, so sit back and enjoy the scenic views along the way.
Location: Maputo, Mozambique

11:30 - Arrival at Ponta do Ouro
Arrive at Ponta do Ouro and take some time to explore the town. You'll find a variety of shops selling local crafts, restaurants offering fresh seafood, and a beautiful sandy beach.
Location: Ponta do Ouro, Mozambique

12:00 - Lunch at Fernando's Bar
For lunch, head to Fernando's Bar, a popular spot known for its delicious seafood and great beachfront location.
Location: Ponta do Ouro, Mozambique
Price: Expect to spend around MZN 500-700 for lunch.

13:30 - Beach Time
Spend the afternoon enjoying the beautiful beach. You can swim, sunbathe, or try out some water sports like surfing or snorkeling. Equipment rental shops are available along the beach.
Location: Ponta do Ouro, Mozambique
Price: Free (additional charges for equipment rental)

16:00 - Dolphin Watching Tour
Join a dolphin watching tour for a chance to see these playful creatures up close. Ponta do Ouro is known for its resident dolphin population, and several local companies offer boat tours.
Location: Ponta do Ouro, Mozambique
Price: Prices vary but expect to pay around MZN 1,500 for a dolphin watching tour.

18:00 - Sunset at the Beach
After your dolphin watching tour, head back to the beach to enjoy a stunning sunset. The sunsets in Ponta do Ouro are truly breathtaking, so be sure to have your camera ready!
Location: Ponta do Ouro, Mozambique
Price: Free

19:30 - Dinner at Love Café
For dinner, head to Love Café, a charming restaurant known for its fresh seafood and friendly service.

Location: Ponta do Ouro, Mozambique
Price: Expect to spend around MZN 500-700 for dinner.

21:00 - Return to Maputo
After dinner, it's time to head back to Maputo. The drive takes about 2.5 hours, so you should arrive back at your accommodation around 23:00.
Location: Maputo, Mozambique

Please note that the times, prices, and locations mentioned are subject to change and it's always a good idea to check with the venues directly for the most accurate and up-to-date information.

Also, keep in mind that travel times can vary depending on traffic and road conditions. Always allow plenty of time to get from one place to another.

6.5.1   Map from Maputo to Ponta do Ouro

Interactive link to the map: https://bit.ly/3r2t0h5

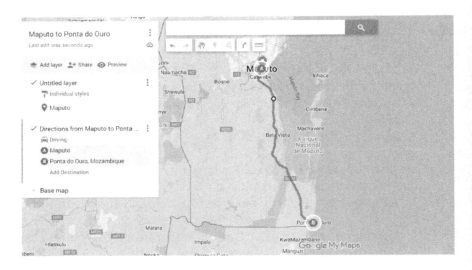

6.6 Maputo: Highlights Tour with Local Beer Tasting:

08:00 - Breakfast at Your Accommodation
Start your day with a hearty breakfast at your accommodation in Maputo. You'll need plenty of energy for the day ahead!

09:00 - Start of the Maputo Full City Tour by Car
Begin your day with the Maputo Full City Tour by Car. This is the best way to get to know Maputo and its flavor. In 3 hours, you'll cover the most emblematic spots of the city and uncover the history behind them. This is the most complete city tour available and a great way to get acquainted with Maputo.
Location: Maputo, Mozambique
Price: $85.00 per ticket
Duration: 3 hours
Website: Book Here: https://bit.ly/3RdLfLq

12:00 - Lunch at a Local Restaurant
After your city tour, enjoy lunch at one of Maputo's local restaurants. Try some local dishes like Matapa, a traditional Mozambican dish made with cassava leaves, garlic, and coconut milk.

14:00 - Nlhamanculo Community Walking Tour
After lunch, embark on the Nlhamanculo Community Walking Tour. This 2.5-hour tour will give you a perspective of the cultural,

traditional ways of living of locals. Prepare yourself to be immersed in the local culture.
Location: Maputo, Mozambique
Price: $50.00 per ticket
Duration: 2.5 hours
Website: Book Here: https://bit.ly/3PqY0kn

17:00 - Free Time

After your walking tour, you'll have some free time. You can explore more of Maputo on your own or relax at your accommodation.

19:00 - Dinner at a Local Restaurant

For dinner, try another local restaurant. Maputo has a vibrant food scene, with many restaurants serving a mix of Mozambican and Portuguese cuisine.

21:00 - Local Beer Tasting

End your day with a local beer tasting. Mozambique has a growing craft beer scene, and this is a great opportunity to try some local brews.

Please note that the times, prices, and locations mentioned are subject to change and it's always a good idea to check with the venues directly for the most accurate and up-to-date information. Also, keep in mind that travel times can vary depending on traffic and road conditions. Always allow plenty of time to get from one place to another.

7 Two-Day Maputo and Inhaca Island Adventure

7.1 Day One: Maputo

08:00 - Breakfast at Café Sol
Kick off your adventure with a hearty breakfast at Café Sol, a popular café in Maputo known for its delicious pastries and coffee. Try their signature dish, the pastel de nata, a traditional Portuguese custard tart.
Location: Avenida Julius Nyerere, Maputo, Mozambique
Website: Unfortunately, they do not have a website, but you can check their reviews on TripAdvisor.
Price: Expect to spend around MZN 200-300 for breakfast.

09:00 - Visit the Maputo City Hall
After breakfast, head to the Maputo City Hall, a beautiful colonial-era building located in the heart of the city. Take some time to admire the architecture and take a few photos.
Location: Avenida Samora Machel, Maputo, Mozambique
Price: Free

10:00 - Explore the Maputo Railway Station
Next, visit the Maputo Railway Station, considered one of the most beautiful railway stations in the world. The station is still operational, but it also houses a small railway museum where you can learn about the history of rail travel in Mozambique.
Location: Praça dos Trabalhadores, Maputo, Mozambique
Price: Free entry to the station, small fee for the museum

11:30 - Visit the Iron House
A short walk from the railway station is the Iron House or Casa de Ferro. Designed by Gustave Eiffel, the same architect who designed the Eiffel Tower, this iron-clad building is one of Maputo's most unique landmarks.
Location: Praça da Independência, Maputo, Mozambique
Price: Free

12:30 - Lunch at Zambi

For lunch, head to Zambi, a popular restaurant known for its delicious seafood. Try their signature dish, the prawns, which are caught fresh from the nearby Indian Ocean.

Location: Avenida 10 de Novembro, Maputo, Mozambique

Website: Unfortunately, they do not have a website, but you can check their reviews on TripAdvisor.

Price: Expect to spend around MZN 500-700 for lunch.

14:00 - Visit the Maputo Special Reserve

After lunch, take a trip to the Maputo Special Reserve, a wildlife reserve located just outside the city. Here, you can see a variety of wildlife, including elephants, zebras, and various species of birds.

Location: Maputo Province, Mozambique

Website: No official website, but you can find information on various travel sites.

Price: Entry fees vary but expect to spend around MZN 500-1000.

18:00 - Dinner at Piri Piri

After a day of exploring, enjoy a delicious dinner at Piri Piri, a popular restaurant known for its Mozambican cuisine. Try their signature dish, the piri piri chicken, a spicy grilled chicken dish that's a local favorite.

Location: Avenida Martires de Mueda, Maputo, Mozambique

Website: Unfortunately, they do not have a website, but you can check their reviews on TripAdvisor.

Price: Expect to spend around MZN 500-700 for dinner.

20:00 - Enjoy the Nightlife at Africa Bar

End your day by experiencing Maputo's vibrant nightlife at Africa Bar, one of the city's most popular nightspots. Enjoy a mix of local and international music and dance the night away.

Location: Avenida Julius Nyerere, Maputo, Mozambique

Website: Unfortunately, they do not have a website, but you can check their reviews on TripAdvisor.

Price: Entry fees vary depending on the event but expect to spend around MZN 500-1000.

23:00 - End of the Day

After a night of dancing, it's time to head back to your accommodation and rest up for your next day of adventures in Mozambique.

Please note that the times, prices, and locations mentioned are subject to change and it's always a good idea to check with the venues directly for the most accurate and up-to-date information. Also, moving from one place to another in Maputo can be done by taxi or tuk-tuk, and most journeys within the city should take no more than 20-30 minutes.

7.1.1 Map of Day One: Maputo

Interactive link to the map: https://bit.ly/3PqYalv

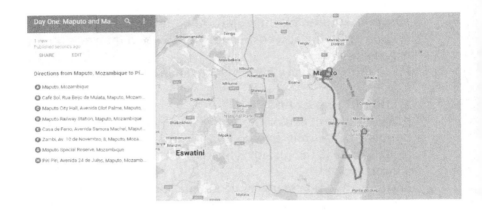

7.2 Day 2: Inhaca Island Adventure

08:00 - 09:00
Start your day early with a boat ride to Inhaca Island. The journey takes about an hour.

09:30 - 11:00
Upon arrival, visit the Marine Biology Museum. It's a great place to learn about the diverse marine life in the area.

11:30 - 13:00
Next, take a hike to the Inhaca Lighthouse. The hike is moderately challenging, but the panoramic views at the top are worth it.

13:30 - 15:00
Enjoy a beachside lunch at Lucas's Place, a local restaurant known for its fresh seafood.

15:30 - 17:00
Spend the afternoon at Santa Maria Beach, a beautiful beach with clear waters and white sand. It's a great place to relax and enjoy the sun.

17:30 - 19:00
Take a boat ride to Portuguese Island, a small uninhabited island nearby. It's a great place to explore and enjoy the sunset.

19:30 - 21:00
Return to Inhaca Island and enjoy dinner at Restaurante do Hotel Inhaca.

21:30 - 23:00
End your day with a relaxing walk along the beach under the stars.

Please note that the times are approximate and can vary depending on the pace of your activities and travel times. Always check the opening hours of the attractions and the boat schedules to Inhaca Island. Prices can vary, so it's recommended to carry local currency.

Remember to respect the local culture and environment during your visit. Enjoy your adventure in Maputo and Inhaca Island!

7.2.1   Map of Inhaca Island for Day Two

Interactive link to the map: https://bit.ly/3Zbd9ts

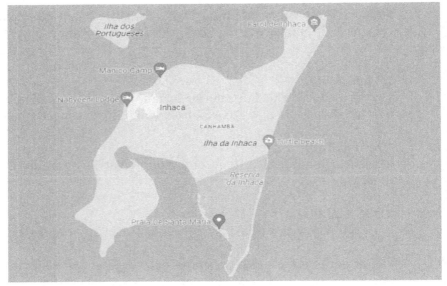

8 Three-Day Maputo and Tofo Beach Getaway

8.1 Day One: Maputo

08:00 - 10:00
Start your day with a visit to the Maputo Central Market. This bustling market offers a variety of fresh fruits, vegetables, fish, and local handicrafts. It's a great place to experience the local culture and pick up some souvenirs.

10:30 - 12:00
Next, head to the Maputo Railway Station, a historical landmark known for its Victorian architecture. It's considered one of the most beautiful railway stations in the world.

12:30 - 14:00
For lunch, visit the Fish Market. Here, you can choose your own seafood and have it cooked at one of the nearby restaurants. It's a unique dining experience that shouldn't be missed.

14:30 - 16:00

After lunch, take a stroll around the Maputo City Hall and Independence Square. These are important historical sites that offer a glimpse into the country's past.

16:30 - 18:00
Visit the Fort of Maputo. This fort houses a museum that displays various historical artifacts. It's a great place to learn more about the history of Mozambique.

18:30 - 20:00
Enjoy dinner at Zambi, a popular restaurant that offers a variety of local and international dishes.

20:30 - 23:00
End your day with a visit to Gil Vicente Café and Bar, a popular nightlife spot where you can enjoy live music and performances.

Remember to respect the local culture and environment during your visit. Enjoy your adventure in Maputo and Tofo Beach!

Please note that this is a general itinerary, and the actual schedule and activities may vary depending on various factors such as weather, local conditions, and personal preferences.

8.1.1 Map of Maputo for Day One

Interactive link to the map: https://bit.ly/3qWBlTI

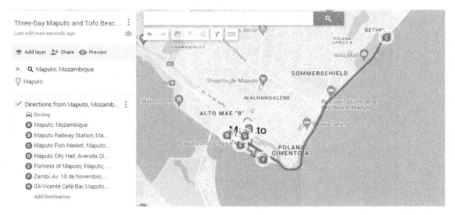

8.2 Day 2: Travel to Tofo Beach

08:00 - 14:00
Start your journey to Tofo Beach. The drive takes about 6 hours, so make sure to pack some snacks for the road.

14:30 - 16:00
Upon arrival, check into your accommodation and freshen up.

16:30 - 18:00
Spend the rest of the afternoon exploring the beach and the local area.

18:30 - 20:00
Enjoy a beachside dinner at Branko's, a local restaurant known for its fresh seafood.

20:30 - 23:00
Relax and enjoy the peaceful beach atmosphere. You can take a walk along the beach or simply enjoy the sound of the waves from your accommodation.

8.2.1 Map of Day Two: Maputo to Tofo Beach

Interactive link to the map: https://bit.ly/3R7KLGz

8.3 Day 3: Tofo Beach Adventure

08:00 - 10:00
Start your day with a boat tour. You can spot dolphins, whales, and other marine life.

10:30 - 12:00
Visit the Marine Megafauna Foundation to learn about the local marine life and conservation efforts.

12:30 - 14:00
Enjoy lunch at Casa de Comer, a popular restaurant with a variety of dishes.

14:30 - 16:00
Spend the afternoon snorkeling or diving. The clear waters of Tofo Beach are perfect for underwater exploration.

16:30 - 18:00
Relax on the beach and soak up the sun.

18:30 - 20:00
Enjoy your last dinner at Tofo Tofo, another great local restaurant.

20:30 - 23:00
End your day and your three-day getaway with a relaxing evening at your accommodation.

Please note that the times are approximate and can vary depending on the pace of your activities and travel times. Always check the opening hours of the attractions and the boat schedules to Inhaca Island. Prices can vary, so it's recommended to carry local currency.

Remember to respect the local culture and environment during your visit. Enjoy your adventure in Maputo and Tofo Beach!

8.3.1 Map for Day Three: Tofo Beach

Interactive link to the map: https://bit.ly/3PwCECk

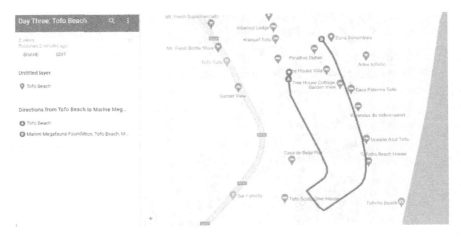

8.3.2 Getting around Tofo Beach

Tofo Beach is a small, laid-back beach town in Mozambique, and getting around is relatively straightforward. Here are some of the best ways to navigate the area:.

Walking
Given its size, one of the easiest ways to get around Tofo Beach is on foot. Many of the local attractions, restaurants, and accommodations are within walking distance of each other. Walking also allows you to take in the beautiful coastal scenery at your own pace.

Bicycle
Renting a bicycle can be a fun and efficient way to explore Tofo Beach and the surrounding areas. Some accommodations may offer bicycle rentals, or you can rent from local shops.

Tuk-Tuk
For longer distances or when you're carrying beach gear, you might consider taking a tuk-tuk. These motorized rickshaws are a common form of transport in many parts of Mozambique, including Tofo Beach.

Local Buses (Chapas)
For travel to nearby towns or attractions outside of Tofo, you can use local minibuses known as chapas. They are a cheap and authentic way to travel, but they can be crowded and don't always adhere to a strict schedule.

Car Rental

If you're comfortable driving and want the flexibility to explore at your own pace, you could consider renting a car. Keep in mind that you'll need a valid international driver's license, and you should be comfortable driving on sand as not all roads are paved.

9 Practical Tips for Visiting Mozambique

Here are some practical tips for first-time tourists in

In summary below are some practical tips for first-time travellers to Mozambique.

9.1 Health and Safety

Malaria is prevalent in Mozambique, so it's advisable to take anti-malarial medication. Also, ensure you're up-to-date with routine vaccines, and consider getting vaccines for diseases like Typhoid and Hepatitis A. Always drink bottled water and avoid ice in your drinks.

9.2 Currency

The official currency is the Mozambican Metical (MZN). Credit cards are accepted in larger hotels and restaurants, but it's a good idea to carry cash for smaller establishments and local markets. ATMs are available in cities and larger towns.

9.3 Language

The official language is Portuguese. English is not widely spoken outside of tourist areas and major cities, so learning a few basic Portuguese phrases can be helpful.

9.4 Clothing

Dress modestly, especially when visiting rural areas and religious sites. Lightweight, breathable clothing is recommended due to the tropical climate. Don't forget your swimwear for Mozambique's beautiful beaches!

9.5 Transportation

Public transportation options include buses and chapas (minibuses), but they can be crowded and may not adhere to a strict schedule. Taxis are available in cities. If you're planning to drive, be aware that road conditions can be poor in some areas, and a 4x4 might be necessary for rural areas.

9.6 Respect Local Customs

Mozambicans are generally friendly and welcoming. Respect local customs and traditions, and always ask for permission before taking photos of people.

9.7 Security

While Mozambique is generally safe for tourists, petty crime like pickpocketing can occur, especially in crowded places. Be aware of your surroundings, don't flash expensive items, and use hotel safes for your valuables.

9.8 Food and Water

Mozambican cuisine is a blend of African, Portuguese, and Indian influences, with seafood being a prominent feature. Always ensure that your food is thoroughly cooked and served hot. Drink bottled water and ice in your drinks should be avoided.

Remember, these tips are based on information available up to September 2021, and the situation can change. Always check for the most recent information before your trip. Enjoy your visit to Mozambique!

10 Conclusion

As we conclude this comprehensive guide to Mozambique, it's clear that this vibrant country is a hidden gem waiting to be discovered. From the bustling city life of Maputo to the tranquil beaches of Tofo, from the historical richness of Ilha de Mozambique to the natural splendor of Gorongosa National Park, Mozambique offers a diverse range of experiences that cater to all types of travelers.

Whether you're a history buff, a nature enthusiast, a beach lover, or a foodie, Mozambique has something for you. The country's rich cultural heritage, influenced by African, Portuguese, and Arab traditions, is reflected in its architecture, its music, and its cuisine. The Mozambican people, known for their warmth and hospitality, add to the country's charm and make visitors feel at home.

In Mozambique, you can start your day with a sunrise walk on a pristine beach, spend your afternoon exploring a bustling local market or a historical museum, and end your day with a delicious seafood meal while watching a breathtaking sunset over the Indian Ocean. For the more adventurous, the country offers wildlife safaris, scuba diving, and mountain hiking.

However, like any travel destination, it's important to plan your trip well. Make sure you're aware of the visa requirements, health precautions, and local customs. Learn a few phrases in Portuguese, carry local currency, and respect the local culture and environment.

In conclusion, Mozambique, with its unique blend of natural beauty, rich history, and vibrant culture, offers an unforgettable travel experience. Whether you're planning a short trip or a long stay, this guide should help you make the most of your visit to this beautiful country. So pack your bags, open your heart, and embrace the magic of Mozambique.

Boa viagem! (Have a good trip!)

Printed in Great Britain
by Amazon